Reflections
on San Francisco Bay

To The finest
Kayaker I know.
Happy Paddling

Reflections
on San Francisco Bay

A Kayaker's Tall Tales
Volume XI

John Boeschen

Contents

"If you don't know where you're going, any road will take you there."

The Cheshire Cat, *Alice's Adventures in Wonderland,* by Charles Lutwidge Dodgson, 1865

Introduction

This is volume 11 of *Reflections on San Francisco Bay: A Kayaker's Tall Tales*. Part of a longer time flow—2000 through 2010—the tales in this volume chronicle only the paddles in 2010. Few exceptions aside (holidays, trips, and kayak-nullifying aches and pains), each Thursday evening during these years has found us kayaking San Francisco Bay.

As for beginnings, the Thursday night paddles started with a mountain bike injury.

The long and the short of it is I fell while mountain biking and wrecked my knee. Sam, a fellow mountain biker and kayaker, introduced me to kayaking. Another fellow rider, Jay, was taken by kayaking, too, and we were three, the first of the Thursday night paddlers.

Why Thursday nights? Thursday night was one of our regular mountain bike rides. That time slot now vacant, we filled it with kayaking. This transformation took place in late winter / early spring of 1998.

Thursday night paddles have evolved into show 'n goes. I've built up a list of more than 100 kayakers who've expressed an interest in paddling Thursdays. I email the Thursday launch site and time on Tuesdays. Those on the list who can go, show. An average turnout is 7 or 8 paddlers, 10 or 12 the high.

In the years I've been paddling Thursday nights, I've had to solo less than a dozen times. That's not a bad statistic, considering we paddle every Thursday night of the year. The tall tale "Alone" on page 155 describes one of those few solo outings.

A standard feature of Thursday nights is a mid-paddle dinner stop, usually on a secluded beach. Most bay area residents have no clue to the bay's treasure trove of sandy stretches, but once you're on the water, they're hard to miss. Thursday night dinners are potluck, paddlers bringing whatever strikes their fancy. If the grub is well received, a repeat is encouraged.

Each paddle report in this volume was originally emailed to a list of enthusiasts several days after the outing. Accompanying each report is a second and quite different take on the happenings of that Thursday: a collection of photos from the evening rendered into comic book format. In the last section of this volume, you'll find a sample ComiX from one 2010 outing.

I hope you enjoy the tall tales in this volume, and, if you ever find yourself in San Francisco, join us for a paddle on the bay.

1. Signs & Meditation

Signs, signs, everywhere signs. The past several years, I've noticed an increase in the signage at Jailhouse Beach, most taking the form of "Private Beach, Right to Pass by Permission and Subject to Control of Owners."

Interesting thing about California is that all tidelands are held in the public trust. The concept that beaches are in the public trust passed from Roman and English common law to California when the state was admitted to the Union in 1850. King commerce is the reason for the trust: citizens cannot interfere with commerce by claiming ownership rights to tidelands and coastal waters.

While homeowners can't claim ownership of beaches adjoining their property (but try to explain that to law enforcement officials summoned to toss you off those beaches—been there, been tossed off), California law does give property owners leeway to limit and control (but not completely cut off) access to beaches if that access crosses their property.

Oftentimes, property owners will try for limited access because of privacy issues, the public traipsing through their backyards 24/7 a pain. Other times, beach-goer behavior shouts out for restricting access: loud and rowdy parties, uncollected trash, dog's left uncurbed, landscaping trampled, and so on.

That said, we're on our best behavior at our launch sites, Jailhouse included. It's just the new signage and landscaping springing up along the access points at Jailhouse that's worrisome. Maybe I'm misreading the tea leaves, but . . .

Billy Pilgrim, Wild Bill, Indiana, the Mayor, and I showed up for Thursday's paddle and wound our way through the signage to the beach with but one minor incident. Left next to a cluster of newly planted flowers, a small dry bag tipped over, slightly rearranging a flowering plant. We were alerted to the incident by a homeowner. Wild Bill, closest to the incident site, fluffed up the flowers and apologized to the homeowner. The damage minimal, the two parted ways with a handshake and smiles.

We pushed off the beach into a Hound-of-the-Baskerville's fog, the Richmond-San Rafael Bridge to our left lost from view three spans distant. Some daylight able to seep through the gray, we weren't worried about freighters or ferries, the ferries not a problem as long as we stayed close to the bridge, the freighters as long as we kept our eyes open.

Depressed by the dreary overcast, the water was listless, flat, morose. We avoided the water's taciturn ways and kept up a lively banter the 3 miles to Red Rock's Toilet Bowl Beach. No recent storms to flush driftwood onto Toilet Bowl, gathering up a small pile of firewood, none of it dry, took some time. Anxious for warmth, the evening growing cold, we jammed Billy Pilgrim's single-burner propane stove into the bottom of the pile. Fifteen minutes, that's how long it took to ignite the wet wood, but once lit, it stayed lit till our leave-taking several hours later.

Chicken wings, ribs, and fancy Italian sausage in a Chanterelle mushroom sauce for the carnivores, celery sticks for the vegans. That was dinner. Though no vegans were on Toilet Bowl Thursday, the celery suffered the same fate as the meat.

The Czar's birthday imminent, Billy Pilgrim brought a large chocolate cake dressed in white frosting and topped with Hershey's chocolate drops. It was a wondrously decadent cake. That the Czar failed to show for the paddle didn't dampen the mood, not one bit, the cake consumed but for a single slice, that slice set atop the fire Viking style. For the curious, the cake did not burn, it melted, poured down into the fire like water over Niagara, the source of the flow sugar, the cake's #1 ingredient.

We left Toilet Bowl around 8 PM, the evening dark and clear, the gray fog gone an hour earlier. Despite the favorable conditions, the water remained tired and listless. Paddling on tired, flat water is not difficult, minimal thought and exertion the only requirements.

Paddling in tranquil conditions, I like to look no further than the bow of my boat, mesmerized by the water flowing past. Mindless is what it is. Not to boast, but I do mindless well. As long as I don't get crunched by a freighter or tanker, absent-minded paddling is mellow, close to meditative. Thursday night, the north bay was free of tankers and freighters.

The east side of the shipping channel to Jailhouse Beach was a blank, a 2-mile-long tabula rasa, the keel of my kayak scraping against the public beach what brought me back to mindful. Used to be a sign posted in my college gym: "No pain, no gain." When I landed on Jailhouse, I felt no pain but there'd been all that gain, all the way from the shipping channel to the beach. Imagine that.

Signs. Too many signs.

Stats

Date: Thursday, 7 January 2010.
Distance: Six point one nautical miles.
Speed: One point four knots.
Time: Four point five hours.
Spray factor: None.
Dessert: Chocolate cake, chocolate fudge, macadamia nut sugar cookies.

2. A Baker's Dozen

A baker's dozen, that's how many showed up for Thursday's paddle. Phil, Zoneguy, Jay, Ross, Indiana, the Professor, Jonathon, Wild Bill, Bruce, the Mayor, Billy Pilgrim, the Czar, and I. That's the largest draw Thursday night has had in some time, definitely the most to show for a winter paddle.

With several forecasts calling for cold, overcast, and wet, the turnout was surprising. Of the three meteorological conditions promised, only one—cold—made an appearance, even that not extreme, mid to low 50s at the launch, slipping into the high to mid 40s with darkness.

A short-term collective premonition of what the evening really had in store—perfect kayaking weather—may have accounted in small part for the turnout. On a grander scale, I'd venture that the group's longer-term collective sense of what was brewing out at sea and its imminent kayaking consequences was a larger draw.

What was brewing out at sea was a real storm. Constipated for weeks, the Pacific was in dire straits, a massive buildup of sturm und drang straining to dump on the coast. Sensing that sooner or later the lady was going to get her enema, Thursday's baker's dozen took to the water while they still could.

Except for two events, no sign of the storm-in-waiting broke through to the bay. The first event wasn't even much of an event, 5- to 7-foot swells lollygagging into the bay under the Golden Gate Bridge and our boats. Except for those swells, the water was as flat and smooth as it gets, our kayaks mirrored Ansel-Adams-perfect in the water.

What I just said about the water? It being smooth as glass? That wasn't 100% on. Leaving Schoonmaker, we had to pass by Yellow Bluff to reach the bridge. When the ebb's on the run (and it was Thursday), Yellow Bluff goes off, a loose cannon creating havoc. Passing by the bluff one hour after peak flow, I anticipated a bludgeoning. It didn't happen, that bludgeoning. Yellow Bluff was a well-behaved Robin Leach of popping champagne corks and caviar dreams, not the fight club I'd expected.

Kirby Cove, 1.25 miles south of Yellow Bluff and just west of the bridge's north tower, hove into sight quicker than usual (at least to my thinking), the ebb—unchallenged by a countering wind—fast as a rail train. Though we did meet up with some wave action at Kirby, all 13 of us landed upright, me the closest thing to a casualty. Turned sideways by a breaking wave, I washed up the beach parallel to it, Billy Pilgrim snagging my deck rigging before the receding water sucked me back out.

Thirteen chefs at Kirby Cove. Who'd've thought that with 13 chefs we'd have 3 identical main dishes: pot stickers. Not just any pot stickers, either, all three servings shrimp. Topping that was the source: all the pot stickers from Trader Joe's. To the fair, Phil added fresh shrimp to barbecue. Imagine that. What are the odds of that happening? If you know, don't tell me. I want to believe they're astronomical.

Shrimp and pot stickers included, we had an abundance of food. Corn chowder, tomato soup, Malfatti, seared ahi tuna, and a mixed beet and whatever else was in the garden salad to name a few of the foodstuffs hiding the top of our long picnic table. Among the beverages complementing the feast was a 1976 bottle of Parducci Cabernet Sauvignon, courtesy the Professor. Numerous desserts, too, the most memorable a store-bought pecan pie topped with whipped cream and a handmade persimmon bread pudding, the latter Ross' doing.

Foiled last week by the Czar's failure to appear and share in the b'day cake Billy Pilgrim lugged to Red Rock for him, Billy did a repeat, the b'day cake this Thursday for the Mayor, who was graciously present. One round of "Happy Birthday" leveled the cake to end the festivities.

The second of the two events mentioned earlier waited until we launched off Kirby. Traipsing down the hill from our temporary camp, we heard what sounded like large waves crashing beachside. Despite my earlier run-in with breaking water, the serene evening convinced us not to worry, that what we were hearing was the sound of waves amplified in the crystal clear air, the waves we couldn't see as mellow and laidback as the late Mr. Rogers.

Don't trust serene evenings. While most of us waited for the calm between sets of overly large waves before departing Kirby dry and warm, others of us didn't. Billy and Bruce both had waves top their heads, emerging less than dry and warm. The wave that greeted me puffed up my spaghetti forearms to Popeye size, the sleeves of my spray jacket bulging with water.

Entertaining as our Keystone-Cop launches were, Jay's was Cirque de Soleil stunning. Pushing himself off the beach into the retreating remnants of the previous break, Jay flowed into relatively undisturbed water . . . undisturbed until a steep wave surfaced at his bow, picked him up, and tossed him sideways, Jay and boat tumbling rolly polly back up the beach. A real Maytag'ing is what it was.

Timing is everything, and that's where Jay messed up. Had he just waited a bit longer to launch, more of us would've been entertained by his performance. As it was, only three of our group saw the show.

If the Cirque de Soleil performs to an empty tent, did they really give a performance? To Jay all I can say is, "There's always next time."

Stats

Date: Thursday, 14 January 2010.
Distance: Out and back.
Speed: Within reason.
Time: Fleeting.

Spray factor: Ask Jay.
Dessert: B'day cake, persimmon bread pudding, cookies, chocolate.

3. Parabolic Hyperboloid Tarp

"Why do you guys paddle at night?" I hear that a lot, these comments from Dennis in Santa Barbara typical:

"Night time on the water is surreal at times. I have never been comfortable w/ it as I have been disoriented in the SB Channel a few times. I find the lack of depth perception and ability to make positive ids of landmarks unnerving ... especially behind fogged up glasses. Strange moving illuminated shapes that turn out to be the windows of oil crew boats, intermittent running lights disappearing behind swells, fog banks evenly lit by city lights behind them, and half floating logs or sleeping sea lions or whales ready to bust open a bow. Wind on a foggy night makes the experience especially joyful as the engine sputters. Now I only trust my well being to experienced skippers on large boats equipped with redundant engines, radars, and chart plotters, who don't even slow down for little things that go bump in the night like surfacing divers or kayaks."

Well said, Dennis' words more than reason enough for nighttime paddling, at least by my contrary reckoning.

This Thursday night dribbled on us with a welterweight rain that wanted to be a heavyweight, but wasn't, it haggard from a weeklong downpour. Four of us put in at Bruno's under the drizzle: Phil, the Czar, Billy Pilgrim, and I. As beleaguered as the rain was, the water between Bruno's and the Sisters—the course we navigated—took beleaguered a step further, it as flat and lifeless as the Democratic majority in Congress.

Ineffectual as the water was leading up to the facing edge of The Sisters, the backside of the old ladies was a tea bagger / town hall meeting hullabaloo. Came out of nowhere, that confusion. Of course, it didn't come out of nowhere, the confusion'd been there all along, probably a byproduct of a season's worth of storm runoff compressed into a week. I just wasn't expecting it. We played in the water only as long as it took to paddle the backside of both Sisters, then we threaded Grindle's needle for a quick return to the gray, somber bay.

Dynamite Beach was our destination. Last time there, I had a four-stitch landing on the slippery green rocks that litter the shore. Enough time having passed for the wound to heal but not forgotten, I carefully leveraged myself out of the boat and pulled it across the rocks, mindful of past mishaps this evening's key to no mishaps.

Many have been the Thursday evenings these past 10 years where rain has drenched us right up until launch time, the skies clearing and the rain stopping once our boats touch water. In recent times, we've credited the Czar for this course of events, he always prepared for rainy-day paddles with a rain tarp stashed in his boat. Like a freshly waxed car conjuring up rain, the Czar's tarp repels foul weather.

The Czar had the tarp in his boat Thursday, but the drizzle didn't stop, not immediately, anyway. Only after he pulled it from the kayak and pitched it upright on Dynamite Beach did the drizzle let up. That tarp—a parabolic hyperboloid—is a force to be reckoned with, it's MC Escher shape in some mysterious way I don't understand temporarily able to short-circuit the wet gray that's covered the Bay Area this month. Not only did the rain stop, but the skies cleared enough for the riders of the ecliptic—Gemini, Taurus, Aries, Pisces, and Aquarius—to show through.

The Czar's parabolic hyperboloid tarp restored a semblance of familiar order to the north bay Thursday night. A slayer of bleak and dreary, that's what that tarp is. But after a solid month of same, I wonder how much longer the hi-tech cover can hold back the gray entropy that's settling in. This dreary keeps up, it won't be long before the entire shebang spins down to a lifeless, gray, inert uniformity.

Ignore that talk about entropy and a lifeless, gray, inert uniformity. The bleak weather's to blame for my dreary thoughts. Once the gray lifts and the sun comes out . . .

Stats

Date: Thursday, 21 January 2010.
Distance: Doesn't matter, every destination ends in gray.
Speed: Doesn't matter, either.
Time: Dreary and somber.
Spray factor: Hardly worth mentioning.
Dessert: Jiffy Pop popcorn and chocolate crunchies.

4. Gonzos

A longer than usual hike—that's what it was from the stairs at the bottom of the bluff to the waterline at Jailhouse Beach Thursday. I haven't seen that much sand at Jailhouse in many moons, the evening's near full moon, in fact, a major player in the bay's low-slung hemline.

About that full moon: it was the biggest and brightest for all of 2010, biggest and brightest because the moon was as close as it gets to Earth this year. Another close encounter of the big and bright Thursday was Mars, the planet's next close flyby in 2014.

All told, a spectacular show Thursday night. The shame of it was we couldn't see the performance except for a hazy film of moon, and Mars not at all. The month-long gray dreary that's been smothering the Bay Area was a thick tent pole blocking our peanut-gallery view of the main attraction.

The water rushing away to expose all that sand at Jailhouse was motoring toward Angel Island, a perfect destination for a current-assisted paddle. Instead, the Mayor, Billy Pilgrim, the Czar, and I ferried at a 30-degree angle against that same current to Red Rock. Why we fought the current rather than flowing with it is as bewildering to me as the weather.

There are two ways to paddle at cross-purposes to a current: the right way and the wrong way. The Czar and the Mayor chose the right way, angling upstream and to the north of Red Rock, paralleling as close as possible to the Richmond-San Rafael Bridge. When they were directly across from the rock, they let the current carry them the last quarter mile.

Billy Pilgrim and I chose the wrong way, paddling a straight line from Jailhouse toward Red Rock. Two miles out we knew the error of our ways, piles of white froth churned up by the tide rip on either side of the shipping channel marking the 200-yard-wide river pell-melling it to Angel Island. Paddling against that river the last quarter mile, we touched down on Toilet Bowl Beach well after the Czar and the Mayor.

Billy and I figured the smarter two of our foursome would have a fire going and dinner simmering when we reached Toilet Bowl. The Mayor and the Czar, however, outsmarted us again, fire and food absent when we arrived.

Tasks to be shared equally, we four set about building a fire and cooking dinner together. The burnable flotsam and jetsam on Toilet Bowl too wet for unassisted combustion, the Mayor did a ziggurat of wet 4x4s around a Presto log courtesy of Billy Pilgrim. Within half an hour, we had dinner around a fire hot and hungry enough to ignite wet tinder, which we fed for two hours before leaving.

The Czar's upcoming Gonzo paddle ate up a fair portion of our fireside chatter. Held any number of times in past years, the idea for the Gonzo is to see how many serfs the Czar can subject to a shoulder ache at one time in the North Bay. Shoulder aches less than a good draw, the event has been finessed into a challenge: Are you hearty enough to kayak to 14 bay islands between sunrise and sunset?

The 14 islands: Alcatraz, Yerba Buena, Treasure, Brooks, Bird Rock, Red Rock, Two Brothers (2), The Sisters (2), Rat Rock, Chard, Buckwheat, and Angel. Twelve of these identified on nautical charts as islands and two as rocks, the total of 14 is questionable. Several authorities have suggested Rat and Bird be considered one island, making the total count 13. The issue is yet to be resolved.

Marketed on BASK's listserv more heavily than Ford Motor Company's 1957 introduction of the Edsel, the Saturday event drew a record number of kayakers. So alluring the event—it reaching near mythical status online—three additional groups formed, each of the three paddling to successively fewer islands: the Classic Gonzo to 10, the Go-With-the-Flow Gonzo to wherever the currents carried them, and the Half Gonzo to 7, maybe less.

A combined total of more than 40 paddlers—kayaking easy on the joints and attracting as many wrinklies as fair—a large portion of Saturday's 40+ were 50+. Representing the wrinklie end of the spectrum was VT Don, his actual age indeterminate, but rumors suggesting he authored the Rosetta Stone a reliable indication. VT, by the way, paddled all 14 islands.

Numbers alone suggest much can be learned by observing others in an event like this. Consummate kayaker and sometimes Thursday night paddler Don't Follow Don taught me about maritime signaling Saturday.

Cutting in behind the docks at Chevron to shave a few paddle strokes off the course, Don't Follow re-emerged into the bay to challenge a tug pushing a large barge, the twin-diesel-engined combo turning directly into him. The tug immediately erupted into a series of 5 short horn blasts. Don't Follow eluded the barge by a paddle length, the tug's 5 blasts nautical speak for "You @#$%, you're fish chum now," the crew's loud curses between blasts confirming the tug's intent.

This type of all-hands-on-deck learning is as good as it gets. Thanks, Don't Follow, for demonstrating a maneuver I never would've thought survivable.

Despite ad hoc shortcuts here and there, the Gonzo was designed by the Czar to ride the flood north to a China Camp lunch meetup, then return with the ebb to the original launch at Horseshoe Cove. The first paddlers to touch all 14 islands in the 37-mile-long circuit finished under 7 hours. The last paddlers may still be out there. We wish them luck.

Stats

Date: Thursday, 28 January and Saturday, 30 January 2010.
Distance: A fair ways.
Speed: Sometimes.

Time: A workday's worth.
Spray factor: Here and there.
Dessert: Milk chocolate crisps (Thursday), Pilsner Urquell (Saturday).

5. Electricity

Charged up is what it was Thursday night, the falling rain whipped into a frenzy by a powerful Lewinski. Paddling from Danny's Secret Launch south toward Raccoon Straits, the Czar and I butted heads with that wind and rain, sharp little needles digging into our faces. Our forward speed didn't have much to do with those stinging nettles because we didn't have much forward speed, that Lewinski trying her best to blow us back to the Secret Launch.

Despite the slog and the sting, I confess I felt energized, not too unlike the feeling you get standing next to a waterfall in the woods. Don't hold me to this, but I read somewhere that falling water creates an excess of negative ions, and negative ions I read somewhere else are good for body and soul.

If you're allergic to the 21st century like I think I'm becoming, a good dose of negative ions can be the cure, restart your engine, fire up your heart, fine-tune your nervous system. One minute you feel like Pee Wee Herman in the back of the theater all alone and weird, the next you're Jack Lalanne pulling a commercial jetliner down the runway with your teeth.

Despite the energy, we could've used a Jack Lalanne towing our two boats through the storm and chop, but the 95-year-old Lalanne didn't show, leaving the Czar and me to face the Lewinski alone. She in a rage, we paddled close to shore where an upset wouldn't be . . . well, as upsetting as it could be further out.

Our plan was to follow the shore to Full Moon Beach just this side of Bluff Point, the northeast corner of Raccoon Straits. Most of that distance we were able to cover in a facsimile of daylight, the rain in our eyes and the heavy gray overcast hiding the sun, already low in the sky. When we reached Full Moon, the lights finally went out.

The light was gone and so was Full Moon Beach. What usually was a wide stretch of habitable sand at this point in the tide cycle had been cropped by excessive storm runoff and unruly water to a thin, uninhabitable ribbon. Not particularly enthused about crossing the mouth of Raccoon Straits, the Czar and I 180'ed our boats and headed back the way we'd come.

The next mile, from Bluff Pt. to Pt. Chauncey, was interesting.

The Lewinski was now directly at our backs, straight on, not to one side or the other. The big windwaves that'd been a nuisance before were now a potential source of amusement. Amusement for the Czar, at least. My own feelings were slightly askew of the Czar's, the chickens in my gut squawking not to do this, to find shelter and wait for calm.

But face is face, and you got to save it. So, I followed the Czar out into the bay away from the shore where what was happening was really happening. At one point during what happens next, the Czar says, "We got to do Yellow Bluff when it's going off at night," and I'm thinking, "This is like Yellow when it goes off and it is night. Help."

You should know that the Czar's kayaking skills far exceed my own. If we were suits, I'd be a ready-made you'd pull off the rack at Ross Dress for Less, the Czar a custom-fit from Saks Fifth Avenue, maybe an Armani or a Brioni. I felt good having the Czar close by. If something went wrong, he'd be able to personally notify next of kin.

Fortunately, what happened next had nothing to do with suits and didn't involve next of kin. What happened next was all about the Lewinski. She was blowing so hard at our backs, our boats outran the big windwaves, didn't give them the chance to mess with us. Those extra pounds I put on during the holidays? Filled out my spray jacket like a sail. I don't think I've ever gone as fast on the bay as I did Thursday night. Might even have been airborne once or twice.

A long mile to Pt. Chauncey, but it seemed like the run was over in less than five minutes. At the Point, we cut in toward shore out of the tumult and paddled to Paradise Park. Kicked off Paradise's public beach no more than once or twice pastimes, it's a favorite takeout. Sadly, the beach had gone the way of Full Moon.

Thwarted but not defeated, we backtracked 100 yards to the boat ramp by the public pier and pulled ourselves ashore. The boats out of the wind behind the concrete breakwater, we found a picnic table deeper in the park, also out of the wind. The Czar's parabolic hyperboloid rain tarp not living up to its mythical marketing specs this evening, we didn't bother to set it up, shivering under the rain, instead.

Didn't have a campfire, either. Couldn't, everything was too wet. The Czar's one-burner propane stove, though, it lit right up and we had a warm meal of chili beans, washing it down with Two Buck Chuck's younger sister, Cheap Sweet and Pink.

The Lewinski had been forecast to get rowdier as the evening progressed, and she didn't disappoint. The floor of the bay along the 2-mile stretch from Paradise to the Secret Launch less roly-poly and, therefore, less conducive to Lewinski-induced wave action than from Bluff to Chauncey, the return to the Secret Launch was fast but smooth.

Except for the rain, wind, cold, rough water, no beaches, and lack of shelter, it was a great evening.

Stats

Date: Thursday, 4 February 2010.
Distance: Five point six nautical miles.
Speed: Airborne at times.
Time: Flew by.
Spray factor: You wouldn't believe.
Dessert: Chocolate bar with 30% hazelnuts.

6. Aging Kayakers

Could have been the difference between Helen Mirren and Phyllis Diller, Mr. Rogers and former VP Dick Cheney, Luke Skywalker and current Senate Majority Leader Harry Reid . . . that's how different this Thursday's paddle was from last Thursday's paddle.

Instead of last week's howling Lewinski, the wind this Thursday was timid. Chaotic waves yeeing, pitching, and rolling us hither and yon? Hardly, the bay was like a bowl of spiked punch at a Young Christians' conclave, the surface untouched and smooth as a used car salesman's pitch.

Only letdown this Thursday was the very complaint I just lodged against last Thursday: a lack of raging wind and waves. Rides, wild and fast the hallmark of last Thursday's outing, were missing this week. Big rolling swells at Pt. Diablo were begging to be ridden, but the absence of equally big following winds made surfing impossible.

I blame the lack of a following wind for not being able to surf the big swells rolling past Pt. Diablo. I do that often, use the wind as a scapegoat to cover up the real reason for what does or doesn't happen on the water. Truth be told, it's aging kayakers and not wind that's to blame.

In our group of 8—Phil, the Mayor, the Czar, Billy Pilgrim, Devil's Slide Doug, Don't Follow Don, Jonathon, and I—2 kayaked with bent-shaft paddles and 3 with Greenlands, both designed to relieve aging body aches and pains. A younger crowd could've surfed those swells at Pt. Diablo using broomsticks.

Aging the theme of Thursday's paddle, we celebrated Jonathon's birthday at Kirby. Jonathon of an indeterminate age, but not getting younger, we honored with song and a 5-lb birthday cake. The cake, chocolate with vanilla frosting covered in chocolate chips, was delicious, the song off key. More in tune with the cake was the main course, surf (campfire-grilled salmon) and turf (barbecued spare ribs). Chanterelle mushroom soup, seviche, sushi, and pasta salad completed the score.

Before a venue for kayakers, campers, and birthday parties, Kirby Cove was a military reservation, the Army drawn to it by clear lines of cannon fire across the Golden Gate Straits.

The fortification of the Golden Gate Straits and San Francisco was a spin-off of financial concerns, the discovery of gold in 1848 the catalyst. To protect these concerns, President Millard Fillmore in 1850 commissioned two large forts for either side of the straits, at the entrance to San Francisco Bay. On the south side, Fort Point; on the north side, the Lime Pt. Military Reservation (renamed Fort Baker in 1897).

Fort Point was completed in 1861, well before Federal construction money trickled to a crawl in the 1870s, 80s, and 90s. Lime Pt. Military Reservation was less fortunate, completed in 1900 only after the Spanish-American War of 1898 refilled the military's coffers.

At the time of its completion in 1900 as one of five batteries in the Lime Pt. Military Reservation, Battery Kirby had two 12" cannons. These guns remained in service until 1941, replaced by an anti-aircraft gun in 1942 and an anti-motor torpedo boat gun in 1943.

As a seacoast defense, Battery Kirby slipped into obsolescence in the 1960s and '70s. A strong conservation movement underfoot in the Bay Area at the time, commercial development of the old Army bases was stopped before it got off the drawing board, and the Golden Gate National Recreation Area was born, Kirby Cove's batteries and guns retooled into picnic tables and campsites.

That's the Kirby Cove we kayaked to Thursday night, paddling through flat water under rain-free skies, landing on Gravelly Beach just below the abandoned concrete battery. An hour into our encampment, a drizzle threatened but was easily repelled by the Czar's parabolic hyperboloid rain tarp, the setting up more of a repellant than the tarp.

The evening a window of calm in a winter of rain and cold, Jonathon, the Czar, Don't Follow Don, and Billy Pilgrim overnighted next to Kirby's battery, the Mayor, Devil's Slide Doug, Phil, and I returning to Schoonmaker.

Stats

Date: Thursday, 11 February 2010.
Distance: Eight point seven nautical miles.
Speed: One point seven knots.
Time: Five hours.
Spray factor: None.
Dessert: Chocolate b'day cake.
.

7. Swamp Rock

When the rhythm meets the blues
The rhythm eats the blues
 "Heat Generation," The Radiators, 1981

"Where ya wanna go?" this from me to Billy Pilgrim. No one else at Bucks for the paddle—Jay was there to help with launch fees, but couldn't paddle because of a business meeting—I left it to Billy to decide the evening's destination (I've pretty much been there done that when it comes to launches from Bucks).

Possible destinations included Armchair, Dynamic, and the Sportsmens Club, all south of Bucks and easy paddles, the current ebbing in their direction. Billy repeated my been there done that for these three, opting instead for Gallinas Creek. Though we'd be paddling against the ebb part way, Billy'd never seen the creek, and so it was decided, up the creek.

Following our obligatory beer-each-in-lieu of launch fees at Buck's rustic bar, we parted ways with Jay and prepped our boats for the put-in. About to shove off, we spotted Don't Follow Don's kayak-topped car sloshing through the parking lot's mud puddles, heading our way.

"Out into the bay"—Don't Follow Don's answer to "Where you wanna go"—confirmed our choice of Gallinas Creek, Don't Follow's name and reputation reason enough not to follow him into the bay. A minority of one, Don't Follow followed us up the creek, instead.

Gallinas Creek forks into two tributaries, the southern-most to Santa Margarita Island Preserve, the northern-most to McInnis Park and golf course. We paddled one mile up the second first, the channel narrowing and becoming shallower the closer it approached Highway 101. The creek barely navigable at this juncture, we retreated to the fork and headed up the other channel to Santa Margarita Island Preserve, one mile distant.

Santa Margarita wasn't always a preserve. Like most bayfront property along San Francisco's estuary, the little island was once the centerpiece for a developer's dream. In August 1914, Marbry McMahan filed plans for a luxury development in Gallinas Creek marshland modeled after Italy's Venice. The wealthy developer invested $160,000 of his own cash to fill in the marshland and create a network of canals. He went the extra mile and populated the development with several barge loads of themed structures from San Francisco's 1915 Panama Pacific International Exposition.

Might've worked, those plans: McMahan had investors, designers, landscapers, and homebuyers queuing up for his dream community. Might've worked except for WWI and the close-on-its-heels economic depression that changed a lot of plans in a lot of places. Except for the canal circling Santa Margarita Island and a bridge leading to it, nothing's left of McMahan's dream. Even the buildings he barged over from the Exposition have crumbled into forgotten memories.

Our attempts to reach Santa Margarita Island were no more successful than McMahan's attempts to make it a sought-after destination. Decades of unattended-to silt flowing off Mt. Tam into the creek have made access by water difficult, impossible at low tide, which it was when we reached the island.

Turned back a second time, we retreated with the last of the ebbing water past the fork to Bucks for dinner. A sawed-in-half 55-gallon steel drum fronting the bar and set aside for burning, we built our fire and pulled together two picnic benches. Bucks still a going concern, we lured several of the bar's denizens to join us, the lure large chocolate chip cookies topped with whipped cream.

Two to join our feast were young thirty-somethings, Mickey a plumber and Paula whose occupation I didn't learn. What I did learn was that the two were remarkably talented, music their venue. Conversing with us, one then the other would lapse into song, the song in sync with the talk, but more poetic and floating on a funky variety of rhythms—R&B, New Orleans-style jazz, and mainstream rock 'n roll. All that punctuated by rounds of laughter and Paula's hand-rolled cigarettes.

Music-challenged, I could only sit back and be amazed by the performance, because that's what it was, a performance. Billy, Don't Follow, and I would straight talk, Paula and Mickey would come back at us with poetry and song. Challenged as I am, I can only guess at the style, but I think it's called swamp-rock, sometimes fish-head music. Google it because I don't have the poetry and rhythm to properly explain it.

Did I say it was a memorable evening?

Stats

Date: Thursday, 18 February 2010.
Distance: Four point eight nautical miles.
Speed: One point two knots.
Time: Four hours.
Spray factor: None
Dessert: Chocolate chip cookies, blueberry pie, whipped cream.

8. Green Light Red Light

Dinner consumed and campfire chatter smoldering toward the mundane—taxes, work (or lack of), aches and pains, growing old, and the like—Phil announces he wants more paddling before heading back to Danny's Secret Launch. Zeerover, Billy Pilgrim, Marcus, and I follow; Arch opts to hang with the Czar a while longer on Red Rock.

Three-and-a-half hours earlier, the seven of us paddled to Red Rock without annoying currents. Now, a 3-knot flood heads north. Figuring we'll be more rather than less exhausted when the Secret Launch finally beckons, we head south against the current, knowing the flood will give us a free ride to the Launch when we reverse directions. And that's how it works: the 2.25-mile struggle south claims an hour, the 3-mile free ride north to the Launch only half an hour.

Three-quarters mile from landfall, we throw in the towel on the lee side of a large red channel marker. Resting in our boats with paddles dry docked, the channel marker's back eddy nudges our bows into its round base, an invisible anchor holding us in place.

Resting in the lee of the channel marker, that's when we spot the distant running light heading our way. Too far away to identify the vessel in the dark, we guess a ferry, a pleasure boat, maybe a tug. Whatever she is, we figure we're safe at the marker, a collision-free zone.

When we first see the boat, the only visible running light is red, a sure sign the boat isn't heading directly toward us. A minute later, the green running light joins the red, the boat having made a course correction not to our liking. That course holds for another minute, then the green light disappears, leaving only the red visible, this a good sign, far as we're concerned.

The boat passes 75 yards off our portside. We can tell by her size and silhouette she isn't a ferry, too small for that. What she looks like in the dark is a fishing boat. But she isn't that, either. What we first thought was a fishing rod mounted on the foredeck turns out to be a machine gun, the boat a Coast Guard gunship.

The small gunship slows just long enough to give us a quick once-over, then she accelerates toward Red Rock. No probing spotlight painting super novas on our retinas, but I'm pretty sure she did id us, maybe with some sort of fancy infrared or microwave, the root canal in my lower right jaw picking up "Today in Farming" on KHGE-FM 102.7 in Fresno, that root canal particularly sensitive to intrusive electromagnetic beams.

(A quick aside, whenever I go through airport security, that same tooth picks up Radio Habana Cuba, broadcasts it in stereo through my eye teeth, which probably accounts for the full-body searches, the airport security guards questioning me in Spanish, a language I don't speak.)

My best guess is that the Coast Guard gunship is prepping for Use-of-Force training exercises in San Pablo Bay, the Czar and Arch confirming a small tug-sized boat sped past Red Rock and under the Richmond-San Rafael Bridge into San Pablo Bay not long after our sighting.

An entry I found in the 6 November 2009 Federal Register describes what's afoot in the bay. The info is laid out under a heading titled, "Department of Homeland Security, Coast Guard, 33 CFR Part 165: Safety Zone, Coast Guard Use of Force Training Exercises, San Pablo Bay, CA." From the Register's entry:

"The Coast Guard proposes to establish a permanent safety zone in San Pablo Bay for Coast Guard Use of Force Training exercises. This safety zone would be established to ensure the safety of the public and participating crews from potential hazards associated with fast-moving Coast Guard smallboats or helicopters taking part in the exercise.

"The exercises are designed to train and test Coast Guard personnel in the decision-making processes necessary to safely and effectively employ use of force from a smallboat or helicopter during Homeland Security incidents. The training will generally involve the use of several Coast Guard smallboats and/or a helicopter to intercept fast-moving, evasive target vessels on the water. The smallboat and helicopter crews will fire weapons at the target vessels using blank ammunition and catch bags to ensure that cartridges and other debris do not fall to the water. This safety zone is issued to establish a restricted area in San Pablo Bay around the training site.

"The Coast Guard may activate the safety zone anytime from 9 a.m. through 11:59 p.m. every Tuesday, Thursday, and Friday, every week of every month."

Interesting.

Stats

Date: 25 February 2010.
Distance: Seven nautical miles.
Speed: One point four knots.
Time: Five hours.
Spray factor: None.
Dessert: A large box of Valentine's candy discounted 75%.

9. Slicker Than a Two-Bit Shine

The launch's time and place, that's the only part of a Thursday night outing known in advance. Prior to putting in, potential destinations are tossed around in the parking lot, a consensus typically reached within half a mile of leaving the launch. This Thursday was different, a destination chosen and agreed upon before the boats left our cars.

Billy Pilgrim was the first to give voice to what everyone knew in advance: "Pt. San Pablo, right? The Sportsmens Club, that's where we're going?" Billy's phrasing a question, but his delivery a statement.

That we're heading across the bay from Bruno's to the Club is a no-brainer, the ebb we'll ferry across tame, temperatures in the mid-60s, the sky an expanse of blue propped up by billowing white cotton-ball clouds, the water slicker than a two-bit shine. Of course, we're going to the Sportsmens Club.

Two point five miles across the bay sit The Brothers, Pt. San Pablo a short paddle away. The western-most island of the two Brothers is home to gulls, pelicans, cormorants, and the occasional seal. The eastern-most is topped by a working lighthouse dating back to 1874, the former keeper's house a pricey bed 'n breakfast since 1980.

Before the lighthouse was automated in 1969, oil to light the lens was rendered from whales, those whales processed a quarter mile away at the Pt. San Pablo whaling station. The station, the last in the United States, closed its vats in December 1971, the last rendered whale a sperm from the Farallone islands. The boat that hauled the creature to Pt. San Pablo was a sister ship to Jacque Cousteau's Calypso. Imagine that.

The seven of us—Don't Follow Don, Phil, the Czar, Jay, the Mayor, Billy Pilgrim, and I—paddle past the Brothers, round the point, and glide through the charred remains of the whaling station, it consumed by fire in 1989. Our take-out is a stretch of sand bordering the west side of Pt. San Pablo Yacht Harbor. From there it's a short hike to the Sportsmens Club.

I don't think I'm exaggerating when I say we're typically either asked to leave or are ignored most places we paddle to, noteworthy exceptions being Buck's and the Sportsmens Club. This Thursday is no exception, "Look at the flotsam and jetsam the tide brought in" greeting us at the Club's door.

Four locals—Jed, Ernie, Jack, and Frank—shake their heads and roll back their eyes, not completely clear on the concept of paddling across the bay at night through the shipping channel to down a beer or two, maybe play a game of ping pong or air hockey.

Over beers at the bar, we try to explain why we do it, being on the open bay at night, cooking meals on deserted beaches, and so on. We give the same spiel every time we show up, but they just shake their heads, probably think we're daft. But that's ok, they know us.

A reminisce of photos hangs on the Club's back wall, among them one glossy showing the remains of a Chinese junk, sunk not far from the harbor's mouth. Above the photo hangs a framed movie poster for the 1955 movie, "Blood Alley." According to local lore, the movie's stars, John Wayne and Lauren Bacall, both frequented the harbor while the movie was being made at nearby China Camp, the film crew sinking the junk at the conclusion of filming.

The photos spark a discussion of harbor history and Lauren Bacall, that good for another beer. History and Bacall could've taken up the entire evening, but hunger calls and we answer, paddling to nearby Pebble Beach to cook dinner. The tide still at ebb, we have room enough for a spread of soup, tossed green salad, pan-seared pot stickers, fire-roasted sausages, and various hors d'oeuvres. Chewing the fat around our campfire, we sound like a commercial for Trader Joe's, the trendy market figuring highly in the meal's provenance.

Exhausting the food's provenance and Trader Joe's virtues as thoroughly as our earlier whimsy of Bacall, we leave the Czar to solo back the next morning, the six of us navigating the bay to Bruno's in conditions as calm and peaceful as the original going.

Stats

Date: Thursday, 4 March 2010.
Distance: Seven nautical miles.
Speed: One point four knots.
Time: Five hours.
Spray factor: Absent.
Dessert: Chocolate chip cookies topped with whipped cream.

10. Hand Rolled

Thursday, what a gorgeous afternoon/evening. Sky blue with just enough wispy cirrus clouds for a spectacular sunset, the sky going from orange to brown to silver to slate gray behind the Golden Gate Bridge. Almost warm the temperature, close enough to balmy to wonder if we should paddle without spray jackets (we did wear spray jackets, darkness when it did arrive wearing a chilly cover).

An incredible evening, mostly windless, too. All of which caused the Czar and me to wonder why we were the only ones to show at Danny's Secret Launch. We hung around the docks a few minutes past the 4:30 PM put-in, but no other kayak-topped vehicles pulled into the parking lot. At a quarter to five, we shoved off and rode the last of the ebb to Angel Island (riding the flood back at evening's end).

Besides a short-lived spurt of wind midway between the launch and Pt. Chauncey, threading our way through the low-tide exposed rocks around Pt. Blunt at Angel Island's southeast corner was the only event to raise our heart rate a notch or two. Not that there was any challenge to the rounding, just the wondering what was below our hulls—and how close—was enough to get my heart to beat slightly faster.

I've not told the entire truth. One other event did increase my heart rate Thursday evening, an event normally resolved by a certain level of skill. Let me preface my narrative with this admission: when it comes to recreation, I'm skill-challenged. If you've been following these paddle reports the last 10 years, this should come as no surprise.

My lack of skill goes beyond kayaking. Two examples: swimming and mt. biking. I've been swimming once a week since 1994. Despite the hours I've put in, I still cannot swim the length of a 25-yard-long pool without wearing fins. Most competent swimmers reverse direction when they reach pool's end with a kick-turn, which involves an underwater somersault followed by kicking off the wall. No way have I ever managed a kick-turn.

Mt. biking. I've lots of hours mt. biking, at a minimum three rides a week since 1987, 12-hours riding an average for those weeks. According to people who claim to know, mastery requires at least 10,000 hours of doing. I've got more than 10,000 hours on my mt. bike, so you'd think mastery, wouldn't you?

Trackstanding is critical to mastering mt. biking. If you can't stand/sit on your bike with both feet on the pedals and keep the bike upright without forward movement, forget about making technically tight switchbacks, clearing tricky patches of rock- and log-strewn ground, and so on. Trackstanding lets you stop and consider different ways around and over obstacles before moving on (sure, you could stop and plant your feet on the ground, but that's just not as cool as trackstanding, cool an important part of sports).

Only once in my years on the bike have I managed a trackstand. I was on a narrow, slightly uphill section of singletrack. Two riders were coming down the trail. They stopped, their feet planted firmly on the ground and waved me to ride on past them. I still don't know how it happened, but I did a trackstand on that skinny trail and waved them around me, not saying a word as they rode by, looking like I knew exactly what I was doing. It was so cool, and I've never had to do one again, that one time just fine by me.

Thursday night coming into Pallet Beach on Angel Island the water was flat, no waves breaking on shore. Yet . . .

I'm angling onto the beach when a sneaker wave no taller than one foot rises out of the water behind me, breaks, and rolls me over. Eskimo rolling a boat back up when you go over is a good skill to have. Without a roll, you have to exit your boat, right it, crawl back in, pump it out, and feel embarrassed. Ten years kayaking I have mastered embarrassment but not Eskimo rolling. Fact is, I've never Eskimo rolled.

What happened Thursday night is no more understandable than my trackstanding episode on that skinny singletrack. I'm hanging upside down in my boat off Pallet Beach, my paddle out of hand. I flail my empty right hand through the water, my fingers make contact with the bottom, next thing I know I'm right side up.

The boat's dry inside, just a few cupfuls of water have poured down through the top of my spray jacket and collected in my sleeves, Popeye'ing out my forearms until I undo the Velcro straps at my wrists, the water gushing back into the bay, the sleeves collapsing to their normal state.

An assisted Eskimo hand-roll, I think that's what I did. It happened so fast, I can't be sure. But whatever it was, it was very cool and, like my one trackstand, one cool Eskimo roll is enough to last me a lifetime.

Stats

Date: Thursday, 11 March 2010.
Distance: Nine point six nautical miles.
Speed: One point eight knots.
Time: Five point two five hours.
Spray factor: Hardly any.
Dessert: Oatmeal raisin cookies.

11. Spring

What a difference a week makes. Last week we were two: the Czar and I. This week we were twelve: Kane, Don't Follow Don, Kuschelaffe, Rosie the Riveter, Jay, Billy Pilgrim, the Czar, Tug, Phil, SF Dave, Indiana, and I.

On a grander scale of differences, last week offered up a stretch of daylight a quarter hour shy of an even split between light and dark; this week, daylight stretched out and fell short of night by only a few seconds, the light of day scheduled to catch up to and surpass night on 20 March, the Vernal Equinox.

Adding to the natural course of astronomical events, the United States follows the unnatural practice of daylight savings time, temporarily adding an hour of daylight to afternoons, subtracting one from mornings. This year our clocks were shoved forward an hour on 14 March, nudging daylight even further into the evening.

With natural and unnatural forces working in concert to keep the sun above the horizon longer, the launch time for our paddles has moved forward from 4:30 to 5:30 PM, that later hour another possible explanation for the increase in paddling turnout.

Wednesday, still 3 days shy of spring, behaved as though spring were already in full bloom. The sky a cloudless cerulean blue; the prevailing breeze just that, a mere breeze; the water buffed to a glossy sheen; the temperature jacketless.

Time, daylight, and weather in perfect synch, we aimed our kayaks from Bruno's across the bay at Red Rock, a five-mile paddle. We caught the last of a hardy ebb that carried us to the rock in an hour, no tankers or freighters to slow us down in the shipping channel, Cujo—quite out of character—giving us a wide berth.

Red Rock, when we arrived, was in fine form, it's chert cliffs even redder—iridescent, almost—against the green mantle of new spring growth stretching across its top and down it's north-facing slope to Toilet Bowl Beach.

Chert, for you rock hounds, is an import that formed out of the warm equatorial womb of radiolarian (a single-celled marine critter) ooze some 100–200 million years ago. The red sediment drifted with the Pacific plate into the North American plate and got all jumbled up into our evening's destination.

Except for brief periods in the late 19th and early 20th centuries when Red Rock was mined for manganese, the island has remained uninhabited and wild. In the 1980s, a developer made a gallant attempt to tame it, proposing a top-tier 10-story hotel with casino and yacht harbor. The top half of the island that he would've had to remove for his venture even met state highway specs for roadbed fill.

That grandiose plan was rendered in short shrift to its true essence, a far-fetched fantasy, the three counties that claim shares of the island (San Francisco, Contra Costa, and Marin) unable to agree on who would get what percent of the take. According to Will, the Gatekeeper at Bucks, the island's owner—Red Rock the only privately owned island in San Francisco Bay—has moved on to Southeast Asia, turning his chert-based fantasies into a more realistic venture, the buying and selling of diamonds.

Privately owned but left in an undeveloped state of wild, Red Rock is a popular paddling destination. Left to our own devices, we typically do a Julia Child on a small patch of Toilet Bowl Beach, temporarily adding an infinitesimally thin and fragile veneer of modernity to the rock's Jurassic-Cretaceous outcroppings.

This Wednesday evening no exception, and with the added input of 12 cooks, the veneer of dinner was anything but thin and fragile, the menu featuring an onslaught of salad, soup, barbecued sausage, salmon, shrimp, sweet potato fries, sushi, and baked potatoes.

To the list of events—the time change, more daylight, spring, a later launch—that drew out Wednesday's celebration of paddlers, add one of the evening's dishes: corned beef and cabbage, this Wednesday St. Patrick's Day.

More pagan than not, we nevertheless celebrated St. Patrick's work, that corned beef and cabbage our testament to the saint's 5th-century recruiting efforts in Ireland. Recognizing St. Patrick's 5th-century efforts in Ireland was only a minor reason to celebrate, the major reason—to our modern way of thinking—Ireland's decision in 1995 to allow the consumption of beer on the Saint's day, beer on that day prior to 1995 strictly forbidden by Irish law.

Daylight savings time, spring, more daylight, a later launch, Ireland's wise decision to allow beer on St. Patrick's Day . . . they all conspired for an exceptionally fine paddle.

Stats

Date: Wednesday, 17 March 2010.
Distance: Eight point seven nautical miles.
Speed: One point seven knots.
Time: Exceptional.
Spray factor: None.
Dessert: Blueberry pie, Inside-Out Carrot Cake.

12. Fish Tacos

Between munches of fish tacos on Armchair Beach, Beach Billy Pilgrim catalogs the flaws in the structural integrity of one of his several boats (for you non-kayakers, if you lay claim to fewer than five boats, you're not really into the sport).

"Darn thing always takes on water," says Billy, wiping a sluice of juicy taco from his chin. "The coaming on the back hatch delaminated and I fixed it, but the water still finds a way in." A bite and a swallow followed by, "Once, the deck split from the hull, and I had to glue the two halves back together. Boats shouldn't come apart like that."

To be fair, what we hear from Billy around the campfire is secondary cataloging, his initial and primary catalog directed at the boat's sales rep some weeks earlier. The rep as attentive an audience to Billy's laundry list of flaws as we are, he agreed to replace the flawed craft with a newer and sleeker version at wholesale.

"I said, 'sure,'" says Billy, shoveling together a second fish taco from Woody's, the cook's, makeshift kitchen, two broken concrete blocks, smooth sides up, the counter top. "Heck, I can turn that new boat around and get myself a better one," he says, a committed kayaker already more than five boats deep into the sport.

Some good (the company replacing the boat with a sleeker model at wholesale cost) and some bad (a flawed boat that shouldn't've been), I won't name any names. However—and quite coincidentally—Capella also is the northernmost star in the Winter Circle, both Capella and the Circle fading from the winter sky as fast as Billy's old boat will be from Thursday night paddles.

The Winter Circle sinking toward the western horizon at sunset is a harbinger of spring, spring having overtaken winter a few days back on Saturday, 20 March. This Thursday our first spring paddle, the day is, like many transitions, rough around the edges. Rain threatened in the morning but gave way to clear evening skies and an unobstructed view of Capella and her Circle of siblings. A moderate Lewinski roughed up the water almost but not quite to white caps and blew us from Bruno's to the Sisters, the current flooding in the same direction. With the current and the Lewinski in agreement, we—the Mayor, Phil, Billy Pilgrim, Indiana, Adam's Dad, and I—cover the 2.5 miles in respectable time.

The Sisters are fairly quiet, the water gurgling and burbling around their north and south ends, but not much else happening. The Lewinski's unpredictability a spring constant, she changes direction when we reach the Sisters, her westerly morphing into a northerly.

The wind in our faces, the paddle to Rat Rock, 1.5 miles distant, is a shoulder ache, the time to reach the rock the same as from Bruno's to the Sisters, but not nearly as respectable.

Firewood as unpredictable as a Lewinski—the wood hidden in the folds between winter and spring—Phil, Billy Pilgrim, and I stop short of the evening's haul-out, Armchair Beach, to gather up some loose kindling visible on a nearby curve of sand.

Our tinder-gathering efforts are successful but unnecessary, Armchair still harboring a fair-sized cache of wood from our last visit. This is supplemented by several smaller stashes we figure the leavings of local fishermen, their blackened fire pits nearby.

Our fire lit and the first of several dishes served—sushi, barbecued chicken, burritos, garlic potato fries, ahi, and such—Zeerover and Woody paddle ashore, the traffic snarl from Berkeley to San Rafael having delayed their launch. To the dinner mix they add fish tacos, the fish fillets cooked above a camp stove flame, the flour tacos singed crispy over campfire coals.

When the sun goes down, early spring evenings turn cold. We linger around the campfire till we can't linger anymore, talk of a late night rain dousing the fire and stacking leftover kindling above the high tide line at the base of the cliff (the rain didn't fall until the next day).

A trait spring and summer share is this: if the wind doesn't stop within 40 minutes after sunset, odds are she'll blow all night. This Thursday evening, the Lewinski was at peace and our return paddle was under a cold, clear sky in calm conditions. Except for the slosh of water in Billy Pilgrim's boat, we couldn't have asked for any better.

Stats

Date: Thursday, 25 March 2010.
Distance: Eight nautical miles.
Speed: One point six knots.
Time: Five hours.
Spray factor: Some.
Dessert: Chocolate-covered cherries and almonds.

13. Downright Calm

"You're going out in that? Don't do it," the big guy standing behind the bar at Buck's says to us—Marcus, Arch, Billy Pilgrim, Don't Follow Don, and I. "You're nuts even to think about it."

"Out in that" was the wind whipping down Gallinas Creek into San Pablo Bay, and "You're nuts" a phrase not all that uncommon among Buck's regulars when talking to us. That Buck's this Thursday was crowded with regulars, we figured the wind couldn't be that bad, what with only one fellow out of all those elbow-benders calling us nuts, the others simply rolling their eyes up in their heads to show disbelieving whites below.

No amount of "We've been there, done that" changed the tenor of conversation. After the obligatory beers in lieu of launch fees, we left the bar to a silent chorus of furrowed brows and took to the water.

The wind, indeed, was strong, but at our backs and blowing in the same direction as the current. Had the wind and current been butting heads, we would've had some nasty windwaves in our faces. But we didn't have any, the water blown flatter than an Iowa cornfield.

The windwaves weren't in Gallinas Creek, they were in the bay, fetched up with mists of spray despite wind and currents traveling hand in hand. Two point five miles, that's the distance we covered from the mouth of Gallinas Creek to the evening's take out, Armchair Beach, the waves building the further we traveled.

We made good time, picking up speed the closer our approach to Armchair. The entire set to was more than manageable, the worst of it being the bows of our boats occasionally plowing underwater corn rows and the less-than-often need for a stern rudder to keep us from broaching sideways.

Truth to tell, Thursday was downright calm, leastways compared to the weekend two days distant, and that according to Billy Pilgrim. Billy, who suffers from a serious case of CSS (Can't Sit Still), was on the water both Saturday and Sunday. Saturday was open ocean, 20-foot swells, and don't go near the shore unless you want to be trashed. Sunday was San Francisco, spray blowing so thick you couldn't see the shore where you wished you were instead of the middle of the bay.

Thursday, Armchair was pretty much out of the wind, two chunks of concrete propped up to keep what breezes did come ashore from ruffling the campfire. These last few months, one or the other of us has brought a log of store-bought ersatz wood to each paddle for fire, beached tinder water-logged from the constant rain. That we didn't need fake wood Thursday may be an indicator that the rain isn't as intense as it has been.

Bratwurst and shrimp pot stickers interspersed with Don't Follow Don's juggling kept the campfire fed well past sunset. Don't Follow claims a lifetime of juggling, his career peaking in the late 70s when he worked east coast Renaissance Faires. He didn't say why that gig dried up, but whatever it was apparently forced him to work as an applied physicist at Stanford University's Linear Accelerator (now SLAC) in the 80s.

"We used to race golf carts through the tunnels," he says, juggling three empty beer bottles next to the campfire, but doesn't go into detail, segueing from there into finding lots of time for kayaking.

His golf-cart-racing days in the accelerator long gone, Don't Follow still remembered enough to entertain us with stories of electrons, positrons, quarks, black holes, and anti-matter, all juggled into layman's language without dropping a single explanation. If I weren't afflicted with CRS (Can't Remember Stuff)—not to be confused with CSS—I'd tell you more.

What I do remember is the chocolate cream pie we ended the evening on, that pie made all the better because it was carved into four large wedges, one of our five passing on the treat. A sweet end to the outing, even if the wind did headbutt us all the way back to Buck's.

Stats

Date: Thursday, 1 April 2010.
Distance: Five point three nautical miles.
Speed: One point one knots.
Time: Five hours.
Spray factor: Enough.
Dessert: Chocolate cream pie.

14. A Glorious Day

"Thursday's a glorious day," she says, an announcer for KDFC classic radio station in San Francisco. I'm doing Highway 101 on my way to Danny's Secret Launch, windows rolled down, inhaling the warm temps rolling over my face. The radio announcer's no meteorologist, neither am I, but you don't need an advanced degree to know she's spot on.

I get to the launch with 30 minutes to spare, but Billy Pilgrim's already there, his ties to the auto shop he runs in the east bay a slipknot, Billy never late to a paddle. Waiting for other paddlers to show, Billy offers me a bottle of expired Bud Light. "Got it from the guy I rent the shop from," he says.

I don't know if this is praise or criticism, but that bottle of expired Bud Light tasted pretty much the same as a bottle of non-expired Bud Light.

While Billy and I tend to beer and boats, other paddlers drift in: Adam's Dad, Indiana, and Jay the first of the lot. Ten minutes before a suggested launch time of 5:30 PM, a lone kayaker paddles into the harbor. Phil, with ties even slipperier than Billy's, did a work-related awol to make the 2-hour paddle from his Sausalito houseboat to the Secret Launch.

Phil's is an impressive paddle, 6.5 miles against an ebbing current just to put in with us. Only sign of weakness Phil shows is to pull out a bag of chips and a container of homemade salsa from his rear hatch. "I'm hungry," he says. "Wanna join me?"

We do, join Phil for a small picnic on the dock next to his boat. Billy's collection of Bud Light now completely expired, Phil produces a bottle of golden agave juice from his boat, "The perfect complement to chips and salsa," he says. One round of the agave juice complete, Hobo arrives and helps us finish the chips and salsa, the remainder of the juice saved for late evening aperitifs.

Five of us take to the water 15 minutes past the suggested 5:30 launch, stomachs fed and minds content, Jay opting at the last to forego the paddle and, instead, put in a few extra hours work before flying to Omaha to visit in-laws the next morning, Friday.

That KDFC announcer's call still holds true, Thursday is a glorious day, off the water and on. The days preceding, and following, are wind whipped, pool table gray, wetter than spilled beer, and frozen turkey cold. Today is sunscreen and bathing suits, that's how good it is and lucky we are.

Two miles south of the Secret Launch following the shoreline we come to Pt. Chauncey. I really don't have much to comment on Pt. Chauncey, except that a few fancy estates past we're enveloped by a tantalizing cloud of mesquite-fired barbecue floating across the water, spare ribs and steak, some vegetables. Lots of barbecue sauce.

Before that cloud of smell overcomes us, our destination is Pallet Beach on Angel Island, 3.75 miles distant. That changes to cries of "Food" and "Let's eat now," our new destination Ferry Wake Beach, a short half mile away.

Ferry Wake is named for our first outing there, the break from a ferry's wake swamping the entire cove, from shoreline to cliff base, putting out our campfire, waterlogging our food, trying to snatch our boats and gear. Tonight, plenty of sand is left exposed from the just-ended ebb tide, leaving room enough for us and a breaking ferry wake, should room be needed.

A campfire is lit within minutes of taking out, food bubbling in deep frying pans on propane stoves, hors d'oeuvres carefully arranged on downed tree limbs. Main courses are a mixed salad, pan-fried shrimp and veggies, a Trader Joe's rice dish, buffalo wings, and spare ribs. Dessert is cocoa-covered almonds, and the last of Phil's agave juice cleanses our palates.

Short a juggler, our only entertainment, besides idle chatter, is a semi-clear blue rubber ball Billy Pilgrim found floating among the rocks just this side of Pt. Chauncey. Golf-ball-sized, the blue ball has "Lawrence Livermore National Laboratory" printed on its surface.

Not much to look at, the ball does have one intriguing trait: when tossed around or bounced off a rock or cliff, it glows red inside. A fairly bright red, the color fading away after a few seconds. I'm not sure how it works, but tossing the ball around in the dark keeps us occupied till we leave. Hobo, Indiana, Adam's Dad, Billy Pilgrim, and I paddle back to the Secret Launch, Phil returns to Sausalito, late evening as glorious as the afternoon.

Stats

Date: Thursday, 8 April 2010.
Distance: Five point two nautical miles (Phil a lot farther).
Speed: One knot (Phil faster).
Time: Five hours (Phil more).
Spray factor: Zero.
Dessert: Cocoa-covered almonds.

15. Kirby Cove

Gravelly Beach, that's where we take out, the beach named after a WWII gun battery at Kirby Cove. We are eight—Phil, Marcus, the Czar, Indiana, the Mayor, Jay, Billy Pilgrim, and I—but we're not alone on the beach. A large contingent of kids and a smaller oversight of adults occupy the beach just below the gun emplacement still visible on the hillside above them.

Figuring the campsite above Battery Gravelly—a favorite of ours, wind-sheltered and a short hike from the beach—is already homesteaded for the evening, we land at the opposite end of the beach, the longer hike from there to the partially wind-sheltered day-use-only picnic grounds manageable. Daytime on the gloam, the picnic grounds are free of rule-abiding campers, we the only freebooters in camp.

Kirby Cove is a good winter paddling destination, the cold, wet weather a check on tourists who claim it the other three seasons. Not that this early spring has been a fair weather beacon to overnighters—far from it, the crowd on Gravelly the first humans we've encountered there in 2010—but we should've been prepared for them, the little pocket beach at our Sausalito launch, Schoonmaker, foretelling Kirby's occupation with its own scattering of bathing suits, sun screen, and little kids gone wild.

A warm day with a light feather-dusting of clouds, a good portion of our eight brandish the right to bare arms, paddling in short sleeves. Riding the ebb out of Schoonmaker, our progress is enhanced by a mild Lewinski, a nor'westerly, she gently stroking our backsides. Only water less than table-top-glass smooth is a short-lived agitation at Yellow Bluff, even the crossing under the bridge by the north tower unremarkable.

About the north tower of the Golden Gate Bridge: there's a wee, narrow tunnel boring through the rocky mass supporting the tower and the old Lime Point warehouse next to it. The tide low and the water calm, we briefly explore the possibility of running the tunnel. A surge pours through it from the backside every 20 seconds or so, which makes it doable. But when the surge does come, it pretty much closes out the tunnel, the jagged ceiling underwater.

Caution or glory? It's a no-brainer, caution and no hard hats ruling.

Only other noteworthy event on the way to Kirby Cove is Marcus announcing he'll be taking possession of a new kayak come Saturday morning. "Whataya gonna do with the boat you're in now, your Chatam 16?" says Phil. "Sell it," says Marcus, and a deal is struck there and then, on the water, Phil paddling his new Chatam 16 on the open coast 2 days later.

Late afternoon in the straits is glorious, fantastic views from one side to the other. Those same views, translated into unobstructed lines of cannon fire, were what attracted the 19th century military to begin constructing a firewall of batteries along the straits, from Pt. Bonita on the Pacific to Pt. Cavallo just inside the bay.

The heavy fortification of the Golden Gate Straits and San Francisco was a spin-off of financial worries, the discovery of gold in 1848 the culprit. By 1850, San Francisco had mutated from a thinly populated backwater port into a thriving commercial center with a population topping 40,000.

With vast new commercial interests exposed to the treacheries of whoever might pirate their way into the bay, President Millard Fillmore in 1850 commissioned two large forts for either side of the straits, at the entrance to San Francisco Bay. On the south side, Fort Point was completed in 1861. On the north side, the Lime Pt. Military Reservation, renamed to Fort Baker in 1897, was completed in 1900.

Many of the original gun emplacements, like Gravelly Battery, are still intact, though no guns remain. Separating our day-use-only picnic area from the campsite above Gravelly is the largest of the park's still-intact batteries, Battery Kirby. A large concrete structure dug into the top of the cliff, two large circular, now-gunless turrets bookend the 210-foot-long concrete structure, which housed still-accessible service rooms for the guns.

Even minus the cannon power, we feel protected, Battery Kirby blocking any views of our picnic area from prying eyes across the park. As is our pattern, cook stoves and a campfire are lit simultaneously, food ready to eat around a warm fire. The evening's menu boasts mushroom soup, salads (mixed green and pasta), barbecued chicken, chili over cornbread, and Porcini mushroom Tortellini. Spillovers are contained with slabs of fresh bread.

This dessert absent for some weeks, the Mayor reintroduces what I like to think of as traditional Thursday night fare: chocolate fondue. Squares of chocolate heated to a melt in a saucepan, the Mayor pours the piece de resistance into the bubbling brew: a cup of the Czar's Cheap Sweet & Pink, a variant of Two Buck Chuck. Apples, oranges, leftover bread, uneaten chicken wings . . . they all work with chocolate fondue.

Leaving no trace of food behind, we leave Kirby Cove as quietly as we came. A small welter of water under the north tower greets us, and we waveride it as far as Pt. Cavallo, beyond which all is calm. Past the water treatment plant on the south end of Sausalito, we venture shoreward to take in the fancy town's nightlife, but there is no nightlife to take in, Sausalito rolled up and put away for the evening.

A mile later, we do the same, roll into Schoonmaker and call it an evening.

Stats

Date: Thursday, 15 April 2010.
Distance: Seven point two nautical miles.
Speed: One point four knots.

Time: Five hours.
Spray factor: Minimal.
Dessert: Chocolate fondue.

16. Hobo Encampment

A hobo encampment, that's what it must've looked like from the cliff above or from the water afar, 16 of us—Bo, Don't Follow Don, Billy Pilgrim, Jonathon, Jonathon's friend Phil, regular Phil, Indiana, the Mayor, the Czar, Jay, Woody, Zeerover, Arch, Marcus, Bruce, and I—scattered along the high-tide-bounded narrow stretch of beach that was Pallet, multiple fires blazing.

Actually, it was 3 charcoal cook fires glowing and 1 campfire blazing. Random beach breaks pushing water to within inches of our elongated camp, we used Indiana's triple, the Queen Mary, as a protective barrier for the campfire, Marcus, the Mayor, and cooking team Zeerover-Woody mounding variously configured sand walls around their cooking areas.

On first approach to Pallet, we debated paddling to another beach, Pallet's available space not encouraging. But Pallet is one of few beaches where hobo encampments are tolerated, the place not easily accessible by means other than kayak. Spread out along the beach like kangaroos lined up under the pencil-thin shadow of a telephone pole to escape the sun, we managed the limited space quite well. The boats we jumbled up out of the way in piles by the cliff.

Originally 17—Sam back from a recent knee replacement and paddling only as far as Belvedere Pt.—16 of us provided quite well for ourselves on Pallet. Italian sausages sizzled over the Mayor's charcoal, Jamaican chicken over Woody's, an assembly line of Greek fish tacos stuffed with pan-fried veggies at Zeerover and Woody's cook place. Irish baked potatoes shipped from Jay's Mill

Valley kitchen completed the retinue of international flavors. Salads and various hors d' oeuvres filled in the gaps.

Don't Follow Don's birthday this very Thursday, a chocolate birthday cake added a sugar-charged energy to the celebration. With so many paddlers attending, that another cake—a cheesecake—appeared brought with it little surprise.

One of only two mishaps during the evening, the sugar-enthused crowd gathering around the cheesecake inadvertently jostled it onto the sandy beach, where it plopped upside-down. Recovered within the boundaries of the 5-second rule, the cake was salvaged, minus a quarter-inch-thin slice of creamy topping and sand.

On equal par with Don't Follow Don's birthday, Thursday also celebrated Earth Day. In addition to paddling to Pallet under our own power, we brought our own firewood, both acts Earth-Day respectful. I suspect more than respect might've been involved, one load of wood strapped to Phil's foredeck, but the majority stuffed in the back hatch of Don't Follow Don and Billy Pilgrim's double, the two training for Reef Madness, the race two weekends distant, and the wood benefitting the two like ankle weights a long-distance runner.

Adding to the double's weight were two tall Tiki torches and several smaller juggling torches, both sets Don't Follow Don's. The smaller torches Don't Follow juggled for our pleasure and the rights to the first slice of birthday and cheesecake.

The Tiki torches bookended a collapsible deck chair belonging to Arch and honored with close proximity to the campfire. The chair a throne, Arch could've been King of the Hobos or an out-take from "The Lord of the Flies." Whichever, the scene was pause for thought, deterrent to even the most aggressive authorities approaching by kayak.

An evening for birth and Earth Days, the water was calm, the air warm, the sky clear. Only water less than calm was in the going to Pallet, midway up Raccoon Straits. For a stretch of several hundred yards, the strait was doing Rice Krispies, snap, crackle, and pop. But that was it, nothing more exciting than that.

The return to Schoonmaker from Pallet was in equally calm conditions. Only difference was daylight's absence, the return under a sliver of moon and quite dark. The second mishap of the outing, after the cheesecake's foundering, occurred in that dark. I wasn't there to see it—probably wouldn't've been able to see it had I been—but got the report straight from the mishapee.

According to Bo, he was rounding a point when the water dropped out from under his boat, leaving him stranded on a rock that had previously been covered. Perched at an awkward angle with nothing to brace against, he went over just as the next surge covered the rock. A talented lad, Bo rolled back up, but, in less time than it takes me to repeat the tale, he went over and rolled up two more times, water and rock not cooperating at all.

Other than Bo's mishap, I have nothing but good to say about Thursday evening.

Stats

Date: Thursday, 22 April 2010.
Distance: Eight point three nautical miles.
Time: Five point five hours.
Speed: One point five knots.
Spray factor: Less than a bowlful of Rice Krispies.
Dessert: Birthday cake and resurrected cheesecake.

17. Paddle Paddle Paddle Stern Rudder

Fist-sized foam floaters graced our campsite, climbing above our heads in slow motion, pirouetting and bobbing in the wind like white helium-filled party balloons. Billy Pilgrim had earlier in the day emailed me wind forecasts for Thursday evening, 25 mph the average, gusts to 40 mph. The floaters were bay churned up by the forecast Lewinski, tufts of spindrift taking flight around Red Rock.

Besides masterminding the look-alike Andrew-Goldsworthy floating art, the Lewinski can be credited with scudding us across the bay from Jailhouse to Red Rock in record time, a tad over 30 minutes for the 3-mile crossing, the steady westerly at our backs. The Lewinski was blowing so hard, ever larger windwaves fetched up the further we went, Red Rock encircled in a frothy white soup when we reached it.

Different parts of Red Rock are claimed by 3 counties: San Francisco, Contra Costa, and Marin. San Francisco and Contra Costa share the bulk of the island, Marin laying claim to the small northwest point and rock arch we sheltered our camp behind. On the paddle over, I thought we might be able to shelter in the arch itself, but the arch lined up exactly with the Lewinski, a natural wind tunnel.

We were 8 at the start on Jailhouse Beach, Jay there only to share his beer before returning to his studio for a long night's work. Jay absent, 7 of us made the crossing to Red Rock: Don't Follow Don, Indiana, Phil, the Czar, Billy Pilgrim, the Mayor, and I. Different boats and different paddling styles, the 7 of us nonetheless adapted to the Lewinski's wild side with the same fox trot: paddle paddle paddle (to ride the windwaves) then stern rudder stern rudder (to compensate for broaching and to stay on course).

A hint of what we feared might happen on our return to Jailhouse smacked us across the face rounding the north east corner of Red Rock: angry windwaves and a wild-eyed Lewinski pummeled us head on. An exaggeration, but it took as long to struggle the 30 yards around the point as it did to paddle the 3 miles across the bay. Paddle paddle paddle curse curse.

Nothing like the callithump of last Thursday, this Thursday, though modest in size and temperament, had its redeeming features. Driftwood was abundant on Toilet Bowl and, added to the firewood we ported across the bay, made for a bright, warm campfire on an evening when temperatures shivered in the mid 40s. Sheltered behind the rock arch, we only had to move the campfire once, a log's length further from the wind tunnel, to minimize swirling smoke. The only reminder of the Lewinski airborne spindrift.

Quantities of food far less than last Thursday, this Thursday's menu offered up just as much quality: malfatti, ribs, chicken, salad, mashed potatoes, shrimp pot stickers, and sushi. Dessert was a pleasant blend of pineapple, mandarin oranges, black cocoa almonds, and vanilla sandwich cookies. Whipped cream for the daring.

A year-round hangout for gangs of gulls, Canadian geese call Red Rock home in spring and early summer to raise nests of young. Thursday, I spotted Desi and Lucy tending to a hatched brood of 5 on Toilet Bowl Beach. A short hike through the rock arch to the island's west side found Ozzie and Harriet guarding a one-egg nest in the mouth of the mineshaft half way up the hillside.

One egg to Desi and Lucy's five was pause for thought. Why the difference in numbers from birds of the same feather in the same locale? One possible answer lay in broken shells on the rocks below the mineshaft opening. From what we can surmise, Ozzie and Harriet's eggs were broken open and eaten by gulls. No other likely predators on Red Rock, we blamed the gulls.

Sadly, Desi and Lucy suffered the same sorry fate later that evening. Overnighting a football field's distance from their nest, the Czar and Indiana broke camp in the morning to discover both Lucy and Desi absent from the nest. When the Czar did a closer inspection, he discovered the eggs broken and the chicks missing.

I'm told by National Geographic and the Discovery Channel that "eat and be eaten" is commonplace, the rule of the jungle, and so on. Still . . .

Thursday evening's return paddle to Jailhouse found the Lewinski less than wild, restless at most, losing interest altogether in us 1 mile from the takeout. The water calm, I had time to conjure up some stretch-of-the-imagination similarities between Jailhouse and Red Rock.

From the perspective of the gulls on Red Rock, the island's theirs, the immigrant geese don't belong, have to move along. Scavengers and always looking for a meal, the gulls feel no remorse eating the intruders' young, reclaiming what little resources the geese have taken from Red Rock.

Gulls aren't the problem at Jailhouse. But if you're a kayaker or other beachgoer, some of the neighbors might be. Not that they intend to eat outliers who come to the public beach bordering their property, but hints less than subtle suggest they'd like to see the beach privatized, "public" removed from it's nomenclature.

The most prominent of these hints is the crude beginnings of a fence designed to block access to the beach from an already paved public path leading to a bluff overlooking the small cove. Scheduled for construction sometime in the unknown future is a public ramp, that ramp to gently descend from the end of the asphalt path to the sand below.

I wouldn't've paid much attention to the partially constructed fence (an awkwardly steep set of stairs already descends to the beach some yards further up the bluff) if not for a local windsurfer. The windsurfer—he from a block of nearby houses removed from the beach—says the homeowners behind the fence are trying to claim proprietary rights, the sandy stretch closer to their homes than any others. An entitlement of sorts. The gulls have claimed Red Rock for themselves, their Arizona. Whether the homeowners behind the fence can do an Arizona to Jailhouse is to be seen. Stay tuned.

Stats

Date: Thursday, 29 April 2010.
Distance: Six point one nautical miles.
Speed: One point five knots.
Time: Four hours.
 Spray factor: Excessive.
Dessert: Mandarin oranges, pineapple, black cocoa almonds, vanilla sandwich cookies.

18. Twister™

Spring's been like a game of Twister™, keeping us all off-balance. Warm, dry, and calm one day; cold, wet, and windy the next. Just when you figure you've got yourself in a stable position with a lucky spin of the wheel, the next guy up spins his left knee over your right shoulder and around behind your elbow.

Nine of us—Kane, Phil, Billy Pilgrim, VT Don, the Mayor, Don't Follow Don, the Czar, Devil's Slide Doug, and I—got a lucky spin Thursday, warm, dry, and a more-than-manageable breeze at our backs going from Bruno's to the Sportsmens Club at the Pt. San Pablo Yacht Harbor. Not as cantankerous as last week's Lewinski, this week's blow fetched up moderately sized windwaves-in-training, skilled enough to push us across the bay but not hardened enough to make the going uncomfortable.

"Seemed like a pretty quick crossing," I say half out loud to anyone who's listening when we reach Pt. San Pablo.

"Yeah," echo the Mayor and Phil, "that felt quick."

"I dunno," Billy Pilgrim says. "It seemed to take a bit longer than usual."

The four of us crossed together, reaching Pt. San Pablo at the same time. Forgetting boat design and skill level, the only meaningful difference among us was our ages, the Mayor, Phil, and I on the older end of the group's sliding scale of ages, Billy Pilgrim closer to the scale's middle.

So why did the crossing seem quick to the old guys and so-so for the youngster?

Here's my theory. We older guys have aged, frayed brain circuits worn out from years of use. Sights, smells, sounds, tastes, and physical encounters are all watered down for us. Distant objects we may not see at all, closer objects we may miss the finer details. Figure the same power loss for the other senses. In a nutshell, we experience less than a younger kayaker for the same set of events.

Here's the key piece to my theory: the memory of an event. Billy Pilgrim's memory—a movie of the crossing, if you will—needs lots of frames to hold all his experiences, and his many-framed movie takes a long time to play back. The Mayor, Phil, and my memories have fewer frames (we experienced less), and our short movies play back faster, are over quicker, than Billy's.

In our minds, at least, the crossing is quicker.

If that explanation doesn't hold water, this should help. VT Don's the oldest in the group. His response to the crossing: "Crap, did we just cross the bay? That was fast."

Memory aside, this Thursday, 6 May, was one of four annual cross-quarter days, days lying midway between equinoxes and solstices. In ancient times, cross-quarter days were celebrated as the start of new seasons, this May cross-quarter day the first day of summer.

We celebrated an early summer by drinking a toast or more at the Sportsmens Club. Ernie, the barkeep, unaware of the special occasion, didn't let his lack of ancient cosmology put a crimp in our spirited celebration. Beer, margaritas, and tequila shots were tipped up to the spirits until Ernie's drooping eyelids and yawns hinted the celebration was at an end.

Taking the hint, we kayaked the festivities from the Sportsmens Club to nearby Pebble Beach. Adding to the party mood at Pebble Beach was a bottle of Reef Madness Zinfandel, Private Reserve, the wine Don't Follow Don's and Billy Pilgrim's prize for paddling away with the race in their double the previous Sunday.

An abundance of food to complement our celebration, my favorite dish Thursday evening was dessert, no surprise there. Prepared by the Mayor from scratch onsite over a fire, his creation blended semi-sweet chocolate chips, orange zest, Meyer limoncello, and dry sherry into an exquisite ambrosia of taste and texture.

What's left of my senses must've been on high alert, the memory of that fondue long and delicious.

Try as I might, I can't remember the evening's other dishes. I won't offer up fancy explanations for my lapse of memory. Graying brain cells and CRS (Can't Remember Stuff), if I recollect correctly, pretty much cover it.

The return paddle was in jacketless temperatures, on calm water, with no wind, on full stomachs (which suggests the food I can't remember was, at least, filling). We reached Bruno's in no time, which is the way it should be, faulty memory or not.

Stats

Date: Thursday, 6 May 2010.
Distance: Seven nautical miles.
Speed: One point three knots.
Time: Celebratory.
Spray factor: Minor.
Dessert: Chocolate fondue.

19. Late Onset Chrono Displacement Disorder

She's white-knuckling the phone to her ear, talking in a hurried whisper. "Probably a neighbor on the other end," I'm hoping. A more likely scenario would be 911. "911 wouldn't be good," and I self-consciously look down at my shoes, the bright beam from my headlamp leaving her eyes in shadow. The toes of my shoes are scuffed and covered in mud.

Thursday's paddle was switched to Wednesday due to a family outing. A rare occasion when no other paddlers show, this Wednesday is a rare occasion. No, that's not entirely true. Both Sam and Tug make an appearance at Buck's, but without boats. Sam's there to share a beer and see us off. Tug the same, though he arrives on his mt. bike with 4 fellow bikers: Billy, Andrew, Pat, and Charlie.

Before the six of them see me off, Tug suggests he and his buddies ride their bikes and meet me at Armchair Beach for refreshments. A brisk tailwind and a fast ebbing current carrying me to Armchair 15 minutes before Tug and the others roll in.

Tug and his cycling buddies are a fine group, on a par with my regular paddling companions, scofflaws all, but with savoir-faire. Tonight, that savoir-fair is given expression in a growler of Heineken they've schlepped to the beach. Not just any growler of Heineken, mind you, but a growler of Heineken on ice.

The only tarnish on their character is dinner. Not the dinner itself—a sumptuous meal of spaghetti and meatballs with loaves of hot garlic bread—but the timing of dinner. To partake, I have to paddle back to Buck's and drive a short distance to Tug's house, where his girlfriend is acting chef.

Hungry, I take to the water just as nautical twilight blankets the evening and ride an hour-old flood to Buck's. The evening colder than the afternoon's shirt-sleeves and shorts weather, I bundle up in my spray jacket and long paddling pants, my eyes fixed on the white breaking to either side of my bow.

Back at Buck's, my memory of the nightside paddle plays out short and fast. Faster than the afternoon paddle. Last week's ramble on memory, movies, and frames might be an explanation. But even that can't account for how fast I remember returning to Buck's Wednesday evening.

Here's what I think happened: The missing frames in the movie of my memory triggered an episode of Late Onset Chrono Dislocation Syndrome, a rare, if not highly improbable, personality disorder that shatters nearby time. Instead of just frames missing from a memory, entire pieces of time are missing from the event itself. It's either that or I misread the tiny clock face on my cell phone.

Tug's home hidden on a dark street, I wear my headlamp to read the house numbers. The only lights on in Tug's house are on the ground floor. The front door located on the unlit second floor, I work my way to the backyard and knock on the first door I come to. It's 10 PM.

Tug's girlfriend answers. I say I've come to see Tug. She's never seen me before. "Uh huh," she says, holding her hand up to shield her eyes from my headlamp. I can smell spaghetti and meatballs cooking. My stomach growls. Loudly. "Why don't you go around to the front door," she says.

I do, hearing the backdoor lock as I step away. I climb the front steps. Before I reach the top step, I call Tug from my cell, thinking it a good idea to let him know I'm at his house, just in case he hasn't got back, yet.

He isn't back. My episode of Late Onset Chrono Displacement Syndrome has shot me half an hour ahead of Tug. Either that or Tug and his group have been delayed half an hour tending to a minor singletrack header. I tell Tug I can't wait half an hour, that I'll be heading home.

Hanging up, I ring the doorbell, figuring to put the girlfriend at ease, telling her I'm leaving, not to worry. If she answers the front door, that's what I'll tell her. She does, phone in hand. I've just hung up from Tug, so I figure it's not Tug she's talking to. A neighbor? 911?

I tell her I'm leaving, that I just talked to Tug, that he and his buddies'll be late. She glances at me, but quickly looks away, my headlamp shining in her eyes. She whispers into the phone, says nothing to me. I say goodbye and leave, not looking back, my stomach growling louder than my goodbye.

If it's a neighbor she's calling, I'm in my truck and heading home before he comes to investigate. If it's 911, I'm home before they can pull me over. Nothing's in the refrigerator at home but a few slices of Swiss cheese and a half empty package of bologna close to its expiration date.

I hope there's a cure for Late Onset Chrono Displacement Syndrome.

Stats

Date: Wednesday, 12 May 2010.
Distance: Five point two nautical miles.
Speed: One point six knots.
Time: Breakable.
Spray factor: None.
Dessert: None.

20. Betty White

"One hundred bottles of beer on the wall, take one down, pass it along. Ninety-nine bottles of beer on the wall, take one down, pass it along. Ninety-eight bottles of beer on the wall . . ."

I got to "Sixty-seven bottles of beer on the wall" before I felt Billy Pilgrim's bow bump into the side of my boat. That I was hanging upside down in the midst of song—one of the few I know all the words to—needs some explanation.

The forecast for Thursday was tumultuous, high winds and thunderstorms lasting through the evening into the next morning. Prepared for the worst, nine of us—Greg, Phil, Jay, the Czar, Don't Follow Don, Bo, Billy Pilgrim, the Mayor, and I—showed up at Schoonmaker dressed for the worst: wet suits, dry suits, spray jackets, wool jerseys, fleece underwear, and so on.

Earlier in the month, Danny had reserved a Kirby Cove campsite and offered to share it with us. Thursday's forecast being what it was and the currents running the wrong way for crossing under the Golden Gate Bridge, we opted instead to paddle with the currents to Angel Island. Those who brought overnight gear— Don't Follow Don, the Czar, Billy Pilgrim, and Bo—had no problems with the change in plans, camping with reservations far less popular than wild camping.

The weather that greeted us at Schoonmaker was downright balmy, utterly blue skies without a hint of thunderstorms. A mild breeze blew across the beach, not much to it, but we figured the gentle wind could be a precursor to the forecast Lewinski. Several spray jackets were shed, but most of our heavy weather gear we kept on, dry and wet suits alike.

Ten minutes out the harbor into Richardson Bay we lost the mild breeze, barely a breath on the bay. Instead of the feared Lewinski, an easy-going Betty White accompanied us to Angel Island. Several more spray jackets were peeled off, mine included, but the wet and dry suits remained in place.

Our evening on the water wasn't completely tame, lines of small white horses stretching across the mouth of Raccoon Straits from Pt. Stuart to Ayala Cove. Punching through the tiny pony-sized cresting waves was a nice break from sliding across lifeless water. From the cove eastwards, the ponies petered out into bubbly champagne water, then did a Betty White glass top table around the east end of the island and down the south side to Pallet Beach.

The tide on the rise, rounding Blunt Point was a snap, the maelstrom of ragged rocks that populate the point well below the surface and cause for little concern. That the rocks can be treacherous is one thing, that they make for interesting rock gardening another. Said another way, we were happy to navigate the point without incident, but we missed threading our way through the craggy maze, the potential for mishap better than a bottle of Gatorade to start your heart beating.

Rock gardening a favorite, Billy Pilgrim hung close to the bluffs past Blunt Point, looking for outcroppings and narrow passages to wind through. I'd followed Billy along this stretch any number of times, and it'd always been entertaining. This time, though, was a repeat of Blunt Point, all the tricky turns and twists buried underwater.

Not far from Pallet, we spotted two tall outcroppings separated by little more than a kayak's width. A minute distant from the encounter, we had plenty of time to observe water and rocks, note any potential trouble. Despite the sun's intense glare and unbroken reflection off flat water, we figured we'd seen what we were suppose to see. Parting the rocks would be a no-brainer.

"Seventy bottles of beer on the wall, take one down, pass it along." It was Betty White's fault, she as upsetting as a wild Lewinski. Without the wind to power the surge, the water never pulled back to show us the submerged third rock it hid. The water so still, neither ripple nor swirl marked the hidden obstacle.

"Sixty-nine bottles of beer on the wall . . . dang you, Betty White." I flipped over so fast, I was upside down thinking I was still right side up before the first bubbles of salt water swam up my nose. Of course, that all happened awhile ago. I've been hanging upside down so long, I've forgot what right side up is like.

"Sixty-eight bottles of beer on the wall . . ." Not thrilled by a wet exit, I immediately stuck my arm above the water, signaling Billy Pilgrim for help. If it'd been me behind me, little help would've come, a wet exit it would've been. But it was Billy, and I had hopes of coming out of the mishap drier than wetter. Sooner than later.

"Sixty-seven bottles of beer on the wall . . ." Where's Billy? Despite my wetsuit, I'm beginning to feel the water's cold. Before I can finish the verse to "sixty-seven bottles of beer," something bumps the side of my boat. I reach for the bump, feel the bow of Billy's boat, and pull myself up.

At Pallet, Billy and I tell the tale. "Jeez," our paddling buddies say in response, "sounds like you could use a beer," which I decline, sixty-seven bottles of beer more than enough for me.

Stats

Date: Thursday, 20 May 2010.
Distance: All the way.
Speed: Middling to Slow.
Time: Two lungfuls.
Spray factor: Mostly Betty White water.
Dessert: Milk chocolate with almonds, truffles, chocolate citrus fondue.

21. Whoosh!

Whoosh! spray flying to the left. Swoosh! more spray flying
to the right. I didn't mind the whooshing, it was the swooshing that
was worrisome, the machine gun mounted on the Zodiac's prow
crossing menacingly in front of us with each left-leaning swoosh.

The Maersk Jewel, new in 2006, looked like it'd been at sea
more than 4 years, the blue of its faded hull rubbed raw with rust.
Out of Singapore, the tanker's engineered to haul liquefied gas.
Something must've been special about this load of gas, the big ship
escorted by two armed Coast Guard Zodiacs and one Coast Guard
cruiser.

Jay, Zeerover, Indiana, and I saw the tanker approaching
from the south and waited by the Richmond-San Rafael Bridge for
it to pass (Sam had turned back to Jailhouse before we spotted the
ship). Some distance away at first sighting, we didn't see the armed
escort.

We didn't see the escort, but they saw us. One of the
Zodiacs pulled away from the procession and bore down on us.
Wasn't a straight line they chose, more of a slalom, zigging and
zagging in our general direction. If we'd been outfitted with
comparable artillery and felt threatened (this is all hypothetical, you
understand), we'd have had a hard time popping them one.

While the Zodiac's moving toward us, we're sitting in quiet
water, waiting on the sidelines of the shipping channel where it
passes under the bridge. From that first sighting, we had plenty of
time to cross the channel and steer a course for Red Rock, but we
wanted a closer look at the long boat. If we'd had any second
thoughts to move on, the fast-approaching Zodiac cancelled them.

Watching the scene unfold from the perspective of my small wood boat had the feel of a video game. The Zodiac breaking away from the tanker and slaloming toward us, the dim outline of a bow ornament solidifying into a machine gun. I couldn't help but fantasize how many points they were racking up, heard the melodic beeps as each point was tallied, wondered what the total would be when they arrived (and what they'd have to do to beat the game's previous high score).

If it was a video game, the four of us (average age somewhere in the 60s) didn't stand a chance, game over before we could put down our controllers. The Zodiac's two crew looked to be high school seniors, born and raised in a virtual world: speed, blazing hand-eye coordination, nerves of silicon commonplace. That these two kids were in control of a hi-tech and well-armed military speedboat amplified commonplace by a factor of 10.

So what do you do when Top Gun looks down from his machine gun turret to assess your threat level? Take off your hat off, that's what you do, show him your gray hair, hope he sees your growing bald spot, spread your skinny arms wide, palms up, hunch your shoulders, and smile weakly. Let him know you know resistance is futile, that you're just another skinny kid on the digital playground and not worth the effort.

You also say, without being asked, "We're waiting right here until the tanker passes. We're not going anywhere." Top Gun's a good judge of character, sees that the only ones we pose a threat to are ourselves, gives the go-ahead signal to his pilot, and without ever saying a word to us, he and his gunboat swoosh to the left in a show of spray and rejoin the tanker.

We watch the tanker pass, run through a few X-File scenarios to explain the need for a 3-gun escort (the remains of an alien spaceship are hidden inside, the pilot of the crashed alien spaceship is alive and onboard, and so on), and paddle through the tanker's two sizeable wakes to Red Rock.

Our close encounter with the Coast Guard aside, the day is uneventful, the opposite of what we thought it would be, the heavy rain, wind, and thunderstorms of the morning forecast for the evening not happening. Early afternoon cell phone plans to camp in the mouth of a manganese mineshaft to avoid the weather instead finds us camped around a small open fire on Toilet Bowl Beach, a full moon wooing the fire's light.

That's it. You know as much as we do, maybe more.

Stats

Date: Thursday, 27 May 2010.
Distance: Six point one nautical miles.
Speed: One point four knots.
Time: Four point five hours.
Spray factor: The Zodiac's whoosh and swoosh.
Dessert: Cream-filled peanut butter ladyfingers.

22. Cut Logs

Zeerover emails me I was wrong last week about the Coast Guard Zodiacs escorting the tanker ship, the Maersk Jewel. I wrote that two armed Zodiacs were escorting the tanker, the tanker hauling liquefied gas. Zeerover's memory puts that number at three or four. More intimate with my memory than Zeerover's, I'm can state with confidence that three or four Zodiacs were escorting the ship, not just two.

The question I asked last week still goes unanswered: Why so much firepower for a commercial ship in San Francisco Bay? With a more accurate and plentiful count of Zodiacs, that question takes on even greater significance.

A fan of the former TV series "The X-Files," I did a Fox Mulder last week and suggested the tanker was actually transporting a crashed alien spaceship and its injured crew to a secret government lab. While intriguing, a more rational and scientific explanation comes from the Professor. Doing a Dana Scully to my Fox Mulder, the Professor emails, ". . . a LNG tanker if properly rigged for detonation would equal a small nuclear device. The mind boggles that oil companies like BP are in charge of their safety."

Post hoc ergo propter hoc, the Coast Guard artillery was put in place to protect us civilians from blowout-prone oil corporations. Normally a Mulder backer, I'm siding with Scully on this one.

Sparked by the Professor's dark insight, the five of us—Tug, Phil, Billy Pilgrim, Sam, and I—talked natural and otherwise disasters on our paddle from the Marin Rowing Club on Corte Madera Creek to Dynamite Beach on the far side of San Rafael Bay.

Talk of the Gulf oil spill segued into ash-spewing volcanoes, magnitude 6.0 or greater earthquakes, and inundating floods. No lack of recent material, we had plenty to chat about. Wasn't just the Professor's insight that steered our conversation to the dark side, the weather had a lot to do with it, too. Rain forecast for late afternoon and most of the evening, the sky was a thick fudge ripple of various hews of gray and whites, interspersed with specks of blue. Turbulent summer skies in the tropics, that's what it looked and felt like.

Adding to the tropical flavor were muggy temperatures in the low to mid 70s. Though the rain never surfaced, the mugginess lingered all evening, me paddling back to the Rowing Club in shorts and a short-sleeved shirt, a bead of tropical sweat covering my body at the 11:30 PM takeout.

The paddle from Corte Madera Creek to Dynamite wasn't all doom and gloom. Just past the easternmost San Quentin Prison guard tower, a Larkspur ferry—one of the big catamarans—cruised past us into the bay. Cruised by, but with a sweet wake in its trail. Rideable, we surfed the initial wake and then smaller swells that followed past Jailhouse Beach to the Richmond-San Rafael Bridge.

From the bridge to the narrow channel separating Chard and Buckwheat islands, small jellyroll wavelets pushed us along, free for the taking. From the islands to Dynamite, we paddled unassisted, the water deadbeat, the breezes indifferent.

Dynamite's a favorite because it's supply-side positive, always providing more than enough campfire tinder to satisfy our demand-side needs. The tides and currents that regularly deposit wood on Red Rock don't favor Dynamite. The sources of Dynamite's wood are the quarry and brickyard directly above the bluff, their tree and shrub prunings regularly pitched over bluff to the beach below.

Despite the evening's warmth, we were compelled to build a campfire. Compelled because among the prunings scattered along the beach next to the bluff were logs sized perfectly for a small fire. A rare gift from above, one that you couldn't pass up, that's what those logs were, no matter the temperature.

On the docket for dinner were Chinese chicken salad, mini tacos, crab cakes, garlic potatoes with mushrooms and string beans, and California rolls. Dessert was white chocolate chunk almond cookies topped with whipped cream and chocolate-covered almonds. Washing it all down was Mad Housewife Cabernet Sauvignon, 2008.

For entertainment, we had Billy Pilgrim's new iPhone. Purchased only hours before today's launched, Billy already had scores of apps, some of them even useful. His the fancy model with built-in GPS, Billy was able to locate our exact position on a Google map and determine the currents for our return to Corte Madera Creek. Photos and emails were iPhoned to several no-shows, I even managed to text my lovely wife, she co-leading a doctor's workshop in Lodi.

Looking back at the fine time we had this Thursday, I'm glad the Maersk Jewel didn't blow up and destroy the bay last week. What a bummer that would've been.

Stats

Date: Thursday, 3 June 2010.
Distance: Nine point four nautical miles.
Speed: One point six knots.
Time: Six hours.
Spray factor: Not much.
Dessert: White chocolate chunk almond cookies topped with whipped cream and chocolate-covered almonds.

23. Watermelon

Thursday's weather forecast was half right: the early evening Lewinski dancing a banshee, howling like a sick dog. Sailboat rigging at Danny's Secret Launch picked up on her desperation and chimed in with their own cacophony, a melee of cymbals and castanets. The racket was deafening and hastened our—Phil's, the Mayor's, the Czar's, and my—launch into the bay.

The small herd of white horses galloping across the water's surface didn't do justice to the Lewinski's state of mind, didn't reflect what was happening. There were just too few white caps for all that wind. I figure we would've been caught up in a stampede of horses if the current had been flowing against the wind, but it wasn't. I'm not complaining, both the Lewinski and the ebbing current herding us toward our destination, Pallet Beach.

Except for a few spots of natural indecision—the Lewinski pausing a moment to catch her breath, the currents briefly reversing around points of land—we made good time, the wind licking our backs and the maneless windwaves lining up for our surfing amusement from the Secret Launch to Angel Island's northeast corner.

A picture-perfect island, we paddled past a small film crew shooting scenes for a movie at the East Garrison. Truth to tell, there wasn't much to see, a few tents for the production crew and talent, several large trucks filled with equipment. Not much else visible.

We knew filming was underway from an shouting exchange with a fellow standing on the breakwater. "What're you doing?" "Making a movie." "What kind of a movie?" "A short one." "Need any kayak extras?" abruptly ended the conversation and, with no one to shout questions at, we paddled on to Pt. Blunt.

Southwesterlies blowing against an ebb at Pt. Blunt can whip up more action than Sitting Bull at Custer's Last Stand. Neither Sitting Bull nor Custer were at the Point, only a tired Lewinski and the last third of a slowing ebb. Passage through the Point and down the backside of Angel to Pallet was uneventful.

Leaving the Secret Launch, the sky had been blotchy with high white spindrift clouds. At Pallet, the sky was blue, not a cloud to cast a shadow, the Lewinski in her fury having blown a clear summer day down to us from up north (that doesn't ring right— summer coming down out of the north—but who's to say what with the climate behaving so oddly).

With half our four wearing titles of position (the Mayor and the Czar), you have to wonder if any power plays are afoot. Up till this evening, I'd not seen any shenanigans of that sort, neither one nor the other jockeying for political one-upmanship.

This evening, the Czar lugged a good-sized watermelon from the Secret Launch to Pallet Beach, a notable effort by any kayaking standard. "You ever spit a watermelon seed for distance when you were a kid?" says the Czar, slicing open the melon on the beach.

"Why sure," says the Mayor.

"Wanna see who can spit the furthest, just you and me, right now?"

"Okay," says the Mayor.

"I'll go first," says the Czar. He wraps his tongue around the only seed in the "seedless" watermelon and lets loose with a blow to rival the evening's Lewinski. The Mayor, seedless, cannot compete and forfeits the title of superior seed spitter to the Czar.

Complementing the watermelon were a summer salad (walnuts, hand-chopped fresh mangoes, and bell peppers interlaced with a collage of greens) courtesy of Phil's girlfriend Sharon, roast pork loin sandwiches (the Mayor scored points with those sandwiches), potato salad, California rolls, pineapple slices, and chocolate-covered blueberries for dessert.

The forecasters were spot on with their prediction of strong winds in the early evening, but they were way off predicting the same for late evening, the four of us paddling back to the Secret Launch with newly won titles and full stomachs in the most benign of conditions.

Summer may really be here.

Stats

Date: Thursday, 10 June 2010.
Distance: Ten point seven nautical miles.
Speed: One point nine knots.
Time: Five point five hours.
Spray factor: Not too much.
Dessert: Chocolate-covered blueberries.

24. Somewhere

Somewhere the wind was howling, somewhere mothers were grabbing their kids and tossing them into storm cellars, somewhere giant oak trees were snapping in half. Somewhere, but not at Jailhouse Beach or on the bay between Jailhouse and Red Rock.

Seems like most days the past month have had wind advisories for the bay. Thursday was no exception. Checking bay winds on the Internet before leaving for the launch, I read that a steady 18-mph wind was supposed to be blowing. That wind wasn't happening when I got to Jailhouse, might've been gusts up to 10 mph, but no steady 18 mph.

Prepared for the worst, Phil brought his Mary Poppins umbrella to harness the forecast wind. Phil did manage to make limited headway with the umbrella, but hauled it in after 10 minutes, his umbrella-less paddling companions pulling away under their own steam.

Limited wind, but confused jellyroll water, that's what was happening on the bay. I figure the confusion fetched up to the south of us, the wind that did the fetching petering out before the confusion could die down. Though we were ferrying across a mild flood to Red Rock, the confusion, instead of intensifying when we crossed the shipping channel, morphed into relatively flat but exceedingly bubbly champagne water, corks flying every which way.

Least affected of our nine paddlers—Phil, the Czar, Don't Follow Don, the Mayor, Jay, Tug, Zeerover, Billy Pilgrim, and I—by the strange water was Zeerover. Preparing for a weeks-long summer kayak trip out of Vancouver, Zeerover stashed 40 lbs of sandbags in his boat, mimicking what a fully provisioned boat would feel like. Watching him paddle through the undulating jellyroll water reminded me of the old TV series "Victory at Sea," big battleships plowing through ocean waves, steady on course.

The last Thursday paddle for spring 2010, we were all surprised by the cold water. Fact is, the bay seemed colder this week than last, and here we were 7days closer to 21 April's summer solstice. I know that changes from week to week are the norm, but warmer water would've been nice.

When we reached Toilet Bowl, both Jay and the Czar tested their mettle and went for a swim. They were like rocks skipping off the water's surface, that's how quick they bounded back to the beach, teeth chattering, their skin a faint shade of hypothermic blue.

He wasn't preparing for a long kayak outing, but the Mayor did lug a 15-lb cast iron Dutch oven to Toilet Bowl. Rather than mimic the behavior of a well-provisioned boat with sandbags, the Mayor used his Dutch oven to prepare some well-received provisions: chocolate fudge brownies laden with cherries picked from his backyard.

Prior to the Mayor's Dutch oven brownies, we fed ourselves from the horn of plenty ("the horn of plenty" a euphemism, no horn large enough to hold that much food): campfire-roasted corn-on-the-cob, barley soup, chips and homemade salsa, sausages in a vegetable stew, chicken noodle stir fry, California rolls, honey dew melon. The evening's drink of choice was Tug's Ménage à Trois, a 2008 California red everyone was eager to sample.

Half an hour before we left, Jay offloaded the evening's entertainment: over-sized glow-in-the-dark clown glasses. Our actual average age may be a couple notches past 60, but those glasses dropped that average to 15, maybe younger. Clowning around and photo ops closed out our stay on Toilet Bowl.

The glasses a better fit for our mood than faces, we continued to wear them on the return to Jailhouse. Only problem with the glasses—there were no lenses, just over-sized glow-in-the-dark rims—was a lack of peripheral vision, the glow overpowering our eyesight. Billy Pilgrim was the first to call our attention to this drawback, he the only one to have spotted an oil tanker heading our way.

The tanker came nowhere near us, it changing course to the Chevron oil docks a quarter mile before any close encounters with us. The bay port to many ships, Billy volunteered to paddle as our glass-less lookout, allowing the rest of us to paddle all aglow.

When you're a kid, you can do stuff like that.

Stats

Date: Thursday, 17 June 2010.
Distance: Seven nautical miles.
Speed: One point four knots.
Time: Five hours.
Spray factor: Champagne corks in the shipping channel.
Dessert: Dutch oven chocolate fudge brownies with cheeries and whipped cream.

25. Phone Trouble

First summer paddle of 2010, that was Thursday. Being summer, I expected a better than middling turnout, 7 or 8 paddlers, maybe a number as grand as a baker's dozen.

Billy Pilgrim was the only one to show at the launch besides myself. "Didn't think I was gonna be here," says Billy. "I got trapped in the line at the Apple Store," holding up his less-than-2-hour-old iPhone 4G for me to see. "If I hadn't walked around the corner to the AT&T store," where he was the only customer, "I wouldn't've made it."

About those long lines, Tug fell prey to one and missed the launch all together. Thinking ahead, Tug phoned from the store asking the evening's destination. Unfortunately, I'd already packed away my cell phone and missed his call.

Billy Pilgrim and I paddled out of Bruno's into San Rafael Bay a twosome, ours the only kayaks on the water. The forecasters had called for wind in the mid-teens, gusts in the low 20s. That's pretty much what we got, a respectable Lewinsky force 3-4 blowing in the low- to mid-teens with occasional gusts in the low 20s.

"Respectable" not because of the Lewinsky's speed, but because she was a westerly blowing directly on our backs, pushing us lickety-split across the bay to Pt. San Pablo Yacht Harbor and the Sportsmens Club. Gentle jellyroll water fetched up by the wind in neat ordered rows surfed us along.

We chattered the entire crossing about this and that, Billy practicing his bow rudders when windwaves pushed him off course. A leisurely paddle, that's what it was, 30 minutes to cross the 4 miles in my mind, 55 minutes in paddle stroke time.

The Sportsmens Club had fewer patrons than we had at our launch, Ernie the barkeep the only one present. Staked out at the far end of the long bar, Ernie was entangled in an equally long Facebook chat with a childhood friend, the friend in Germany. "How many Facebook friends you got?" we ask. "One," says Ernie. Not wanting to disturb Ernie, we went to pour our own draft beer.

Pouring draft beer is an art, one we lacked. Instead of beer, we got foam. Lots of foam. Readying ourselves to drag Ernie away from his computer, Bonnie, a local, happened into the Club, saw our dilemma, and drew two perfect glasses of Samuel Adams Summer Ale. An excellent draw, no more than a whisper of creamy white foam rode our upper lips after the first sip.

Bonnie-poured beer downed as easily as our crossing, we turned to our earlier mis-pours and found the wait the cure, the glasses half full of amber liquid topped by a thin wisp of foam. Just as we set those glasses down on the counter empty, Don't Follow Don and Ediko sauntered into the Club.

iPhones and long lines weren't grounds for their late arrival, Don't Follow Don more often than not late for Thursday night paddles. That he chose the right destination from among several possibilities I attribute to his skills in reading the weather, the westerly Lewinsky and the warm summer temps clearly pointing to the Sportsmens Club.

We poured a perfect draft each for Don't Follow Don and Ediko, perfect showing itself in more ale than foam. After beer, we typically paddle a quarter mile west to Pebble Beach for dinner and a campfire. Sand still visible on the horseshoe beach immediately adjacent to the harbor, we rousted Ernie to call Eric, harbor master and owner, and ask if we could settle there.

Eric's permission granted, we lit a cozy fire at the end of Harbor Beach next to a rocky bluff. Few fires here in pastimes, tinder abounded, most promising a very combustible withered and forlorn Christmas tree, minus decorations. Over a dinner of pan-fried garlic potatoes with string beans, California rolls, chicken potato salad, and homemade brownies (thanks, Marie), we watched the tide slowly inch its way toward the campfire.

"Don't sweat it," I said, "the water'll never get that high." At 9 PM, the fire flickered out, drowned in bay water. Another thing I said was, "The wind'll be no problem. It'll die down after sunset."

The paddle back to Bruno's was a slog, nearly two hours in the crossing. Only respite from the constant blow was a close encounter with a large, free-floating anchor buoy, momentarily backlit by the nearly full moon as it briefly peeked out from behind a high fog cover. We figured the buoy broke loose from its mooring at McNears Quarry, but couldn't be sure.

That nearly full moon, responsible for the high tide that doused our fire and our buoy sighting, also was responsible for cutting a quarter mile of shoulder ache from our return paddle. The high tide it caused breached Bruno's breakwater in a spot just wide enough for our kayaks to pass over, hull bottoms lightly scraping submerged riprap.

For a first summer paddle, I'm not complaining. It may sound like I am, but I'm not.

Stats

Date: Thursday, 24 June 2010.
Distance: Seven point four nautical miles.
Speed: One point three knots.
Time: Five point five hours.
Spray factor: Less than you'd think.
Dessert: Homemade chocolate brownies.

26. Puppy Dog Tail

The beam of Fox Mulder's FBI-issue flashlight, that's how bright the heavens were Thursday evening. The sky was so bright with starlight you couldn't make out individual constellations. Only comparison I can make is sky watching in the deep dessert on a clear night.

Thursday night's spectacle was the doings of a feisty Lewinsky, seven of us—Phil, Dennis (first time paddling with us), Billy Pilgrim, John V (second time paddling with us), Indiana, Tug, and I—kayaking under the glow between Buck's and Armchair Beach. The Lewinsky had tempered her howl, her voice as soft as a puppy dog's tail, but her blow was wagging nonstop.

A kite surfer launching off the salt grass a hundred yards to the north before we put in was testament to the Lewinsky's true mindset. His parasail was airborne the moment he released it, no stuttering in the air, the surfer a blur seconds later when he flew off the tall grass into the mouth of Gallinas Creek.

The blow at our backs was less a paddling attractant than the water in the salt grass, so infrequently do we paddle here when the tide floods the marsh, making it navigable. Foregoing speed for exploration, we paddled into the grass, a high loose weave of green carpet.

The contrast with paddling in open water was striking, the tall thin blades of salt grass whispering against our hulls, paddle blades pushing off the grass our primary source of forward motion. In no hurry for the bay's open water, we navigated our way through the grass till we came to a narrow channel cutting inland.

We followed one another up the channel single file, tall slender stalks marking the sides. The channel ran a circuitous route past Jake's Island in the general direction of Back Ranch Meadows campground in China Camp State Park.

We paddled a fair distance, the channel narrowing so much that Billy Pilgrim and I turned our boats around while we could and paddled backwards. Our intent was to be bow out when we reached the end of the line. An intelligent move, if I say so myself, but unnecessary. When we eventually decided to return to open water (having got nowhere near Back Ranch Meadows), none of the other three, including Indiana and John V in their long triple, had problems reversing direction.

The salt grass and the channel were Lewinsky free, lying in the wind shadow of China Camp. One hundred yards beyond the salt grass and the wind shadow, the wind was blowing a tantrum. Two factors, however, made the paddle manageable: 1) the wind was at our backs and 2) the water was slack, the windwaves small and trouble free.

The 2 miles from the channel to Armchair raced by. More aggressive winds have, in pastimes, pushed us past China Camp's shoreline, but the water's usually been more turbulent, muddling forward motion. Thursday's water relatively flat, we skimmed along faster than billiard balls on a slate table.

I'll be the first to admit I tend to exaggerate paddling speed. I can't help it. It might have something to do with aging, but let's not go down that creek. To compensate, I've offset lack of physical prowess by looking not much further beyond my bow when putting paddle to water.

Close to the boat, water appears to race by regardless of how fast the kayak's actually moving. Fact is, you can be losing ground against a strong headwind but still have the sensation of forward motion if you look no further than your bow. After all, it's the sensation of kayaking—not the destination—that counts.

Our destination was Armchair Beach, but before arriving we broke with the wind and took out at nearby China Camp Beach to gather up a load of new downfall. The downed branches more intertwined and cumbersome than a Mormon family tree, Billy

Pilgrim and I had no option other than balancing them on our foredecks for the short paddle to Armchair.

Arriving dry, the branches added to a bright, long-lasting fire, "long-lasting" coinciding with astronomical twilight (as dark as it's going to get). Sated with fish 'n chips, sausage, ribs, chicken potato salad, California rolls, Milano cookies, fruit pie, and fried bananas with marshmallows and white chocolate chips, we put in for the return to Buck's.

The first 1.5 miles were wind free, enjoyable even though we were paddling against an ebb. A rule of thumb on the bay is this: If 40 minutes after sunset wind is absent, windless is what it'll remain. The second and final 1.5 miles was an exception to that rule, the same Lewinsky that cleared the sky of cloud cover slamming face first into us.

A slog into Buck's is what it was, but a gorgeous one.

Stats

Date: Thursday, 1 July 2010.
Distance: Six point one nautical miles.
Speed: One point two knots.
Time: Five hours.
Spray factor: Minimal.
Dessert: Milano cookies, fruit pie, and fried bananas with marshmallows and white chocolate chips.

27. A Minimalist at the Minimum

A minimalist at minimum, that's what I am. Winter paddling, I dress for cold immersion: wetsuit, wool jersey, knee-high boots. I don't bring any summertime clothes. Summer paddling, I dress for warm immersion: shorts, short-sleeve shirt, ankle-high booties. I don't bring any winter clothes.

My minimalist attitude is changing, which suited this Thursday just fine. Leaving San Rafael for the launch at Schoonmaker in Sausalito, the sky was clear, temps in the low 70s, imperceptible wind. At Schoonmaker, the temperature wasn't much different, somewhere in the mid 60s. What was different was a low-hanging fog and a banshee of a Lewinsky howling a constant 30 mph.

The overall weather somewhat adrift from past years, I think that's what's causing me to shed my minimalist skin. This Thursday I tossed a winter wetsuit and wool jersey in amongst my summer gear, just in case. Wasn't 10 minutes after parking at Schoonmaker that I stripped out of my summer paddling togs into my winter outfit.

Of the 7 of us—Dennis, Billy Pilgrim, Jay, Jonathon, Indiana, Hobo, and me—Hobo hadn't yet conceded to the bay's whimsical weather, him having to borrow a spare dry top from Billy Pilgrim to cover his cotton-thin shirt.

"Where to go" was the topic of conversation at Schoonmaker once we'd adjusted our gear. A short paddle to Kayak Kamp on Angel Island was agreed upon, Billy Pilgrim the only contrary voice, countering with, "It'll calm down the minute we leave the harbor. It always calms down Thursdays once we're on the water."

Billy Pilgrim was wrong. It took 5 minutes after we left Schoonmaker before the Lewinsky blew herself out, a candle stub with no wick, Hobo shedding his borrowed dry top, others of us peeling off layers to stay cool. Without the Lewinsky to rouse its passions, the water flatlined, calm as the Dalai Lama in meditation.

The abrupt turnabout well before we reached Kayak Kamp, we agreed to paddle up Raccoon Straits past the Kamp, continuing on around the island to Pallet Beach on the south side. Calm followed us as far as Blunt Pt. on Angel's southeast corner, where the Lewinsky was lying in wait for us.

The Lewinsky hadn't left, simply altered her course. Blowing out of the north when we first encountered her at Schoonmaker, she now was imitating a wind tunnel, blowing under the Golden Gate Bridge from the west past Pallet Beach on her way to rendezvous with the East Bay.

Before rounding Blunt, we changed from our summer togs back into our winter gear, horses with flying white manes stampeding past Pallet in mad pursuit of the Lewinsky. We reached Pallet thoroughly soaked, a campfire our first priority.

Pallet thin as a rail, we built the fire between the big wood pallet and the bluff, the waterline already high and inching higher. Fact is, the evening's activities were limited to the pallet's relatively flat surface and the square of sand between it and the bluff. Serving a dual purpose, at evening's end the pallet was home to Billy Pilgrim's overnite camping gear, the rest of the beach in flood.

An historical aside: The wood pallet at the east end of the beach where we camp is not the beach's namesake. The wood shipping pallet that gives the beach its name is at the west end of the sandy stretch, it anchored in its present location as far back as I can remember. The pallet I write about in these reports washed ashore only 4 or 5 years ago.

Despite the cramped conditions, we managed to cook up a fine feast. Blackened egg rolls, a mixed salad, buttered corn-on-the-cob, chicken potato salad, chicken wings, and a variety of finger foods. Extra large peanut butter chocolate chip cookies topped with whipped cream and a dribble of Jaegermeister liqueur was our high-end dessert. We had no low-end desserts.

Leaving Billy Pilgrim to the pallet, we 6 put into a stampede of white horses at 10 PM. The stampede wearing horse blinders, it ran a straight course, diverging neither left nor right. Just past Perl's Beach on the west end of the island we paddled into calm water, which we followed back to Schoonmaker.

Only diversion on the return was a drop-by to Phil's houseboat, a paddle rap on his bedroom hull bringing him to an open porthole. Phil did the family thing this Thursday, his daughter and son-in-law visiting from out of town.

The Cruising Club a half dozen strokes from Phil's, I paddled over, attracted by the lights and music. Up close, I could see a crowd inside, men and women, senior gals in summer dresses. I shouted to my buddies to paddle over, but got no response, senior gals in summer dresses perhaps the reason.

I've heard that it's not how old you are, but how you are old. Whatever. I paddled away from the club and those summer dresses to rejoin my friends at Schoonmaker for the takeout and home.

Stats

Date: Thursday, 8 July 2010.
Distance: Eight point eight nautical miles.
Speed: One point five knots.
Time: Six hours.
Spray factor: Lots on Angel Island's backside.
Dessert: Extra large peanut butter chocolate chip cookies topped with whipped cream and a dribble of Jaegermeister liqueur.

28. Lights Out

After Thursday's paddle, Indiana and I went online and bought "Ship Finder," an iPhone app. Dennis, Jay, first-time Thurseve paddler Wootton, and Devil's Slide Doug might've done the same, but I can't confirm they did. What "Ship Finder" does is track the path of ships in San Francisco Bay in real time.

Tracking ships with fancy software during fog-free daylight hours isn't a high priority for us, the big ships easily spotted, even miles away. Nighttime tracking's a whole different carton of light bulbs, especially when the bay's primary light source is a thin slice of new moon.

Paddling back from Red Rock to Jailhouse along the Richmond-San Rafael Bridge Thursday night, we were paying attention, we really were. Scanning north and south for freighters and tankers is how we were paying attention. Alert as we were, we missed the big dark.

The bad news is we probably could've saved the $5 price tag for "Ship Finder" if Billy Pilgrim had been on the paddle. But he wasn't. I've heard tell birds unerringly know which direction to fly because they've got a compass built into their heads. That Billy Pilgrim can unerringly spot a distant ship at night when no one else can leads me to believe he's got radar built into his noggin. But that built-in radar doesn't do any good when Billy's absent.

The good news is the big freighter, darker than night, passed under the bridge 100 yards behind us. The white light on the stern of the retreating vessel was how we knew it had crossed our path. Approaching the bridge, the freighter's bow-mounted red and green running lights should've been visible, but they weren't. That six of us missed those running lights makes me wonder if they were lit at all.

The flip side of not seeing the freighter was that we didn't have to stop and wait for it to pass in front of us. Stopping was a potential upset, a southerly breeze crossing our bows and blowing us here and there in roly-poly water, conditions better handled by forward paddling than stationary sitting.

The freighter wasn't well lit, but the Richmond-San Rafael Bridge was, light from its arc lamps spilling onto the bay, milk from a bottle. Paddling outside the spill hid the bucking water as it had the freighter, prompting us, in part, to stick close to the well-lit and readable water by the bridge.

Jay was another reason we hugged the bridge. A few minutes past sunset, he left us on Toilet Bowl Beach for an early return to Jailhouse. Wasn't long after leaving Red Rock that the ebb grabbed hold of his boat and dragged him south away from the bridge, off his westerly course. We watched him correct, ferry against the ebb, then get pulled south again. This went on till the light dimmed and we lost him to dusk.

I'm making Thursday night out to be an episode from "Raiders of the Lost Ark." It wasn't, any more than I'm a Harrison Ford look-alike, though I imagine a few hair plugs and slap of cosmetic surgery couldn't hurt.

All told, the outing was quite mellow, with the exception of the freighter and our roly-poly return. The launch at Jailhouse found clear skies and warm temps, the beach thronged with sun worshippers and dogs enough to populate an Indiana Jones movie. Six of us paddled to Red Rock, but seven of us met up at Jailhouse, the seventh, David K, there to test paddle my wood Arctic Tern and no more.

The Tern wasn't the only wood boat this evening, contrary to most outings where wood's in the minority. Of our lot's five boats, three were wood and one a skin-on-frame, a Kevlar Mariner II the sole modern. Wood paddles, usually in the minority, fared equally well, three of six paddles hand-carved Greenlands, the remaining three carbon fiber.

Except for our modern carbon fiber, Kevlar, and cell phones—which get excellent phone and Internet reception on the bay, a working version of "Ship Finder" now at the ready wherever we go—if the evening'd been an Indiana Jones movie, we could've been cast as primitives.

The evening wasn't an Indiana Jones movie, though that probably doesn't alter the character of the players. Of course, that could change with a few well-placed hair plugs . . .

Stats

Date: Thursday, 15 July 2010.
Distance: Six point one nautical miles.
Speed: One point three knots.
Time: Four point seven five hours.
Spray factor: Definitely.
Dessert: Chocolate chip cookies and homemade scratch brownies.

29. Dog days of Summer

The dog days of summer are here, the time of year when the dog star, Sirius, cozies up to the sun, the two a bright, hot glare in the sky. I'd blame that glare for what I did, but I can't. It was my fault, I saw it coming.

Out of Bruno's on a windy evening, seven of us—Sam, Phil, Indiana, the Czar, Don't Follow Don, the Mayor, and I—paddle to Armchair Beach. On the way, we pay a visit to The Sisters, the wind increasing 2 or 3 notches around the old ladies, their white petticoats dancing.

Coming in from the south on a half-hearted flood, the wind shifts into overdrive, it consorting with the flood to shoot us by Myrtle towards the eye of Grindle's needle. The eye of Grindle's needle is a rocky outcropping on Grindle's north face, just wide enough for a kayak to pass through, less so when the water's high at flood.

The water's breakdancing through the eye of Grindle's needle, the lady's petticoats flirting with the rocks on either side. Most times, you have to paddle to pass through the eye. Not today, the wind and flood doing all the work.

I paddle in front of the eye, align my Tern so the current will carry me through, then hoist my paddle out of the water and hold it so it forms a T with my body at face level. Big mistake.

Midway through the short shoot, the ends of both blades scrape against the rough rock walls. The section of paddle between my hands is pushed between my grinning lips, up against my front teeth.

I don't see my life pass before my eyes, but I do see all those miserable hours I've spent quaking in the dentist's chair. Even a frame or two of the future is exposed on that roll of film, me at the orthodontist having my teeth realigned, then me doing manual labor to pay the bill. It's a PowerPoint slide show I don't want to see.

The slideshow is brief, waaaay less than a second, matching exactly the length of time the paddle hangs between those rock walls, against my two front teeth, before it breaks free. No damage is done, no orthodontics in my future. I'm a lucky fellow.

Three of Thursday night's scatter of paddlers (we did get somewhat separated by the wind) recently returned from two weeks kayaking through the islands north of Vancouver: the Mayor, Don't Follow Don, and the Czar.

I assume they paddled, don't know for sure. Sitting around the campfire on Armchair, it isn't tales of paddling I hear, it's poetry. From what I can gather, the group's two-week jaunt was a workshop in creative rhyming. Neither the Czar nor Don't Follow Don offer up any of their creations, but the Mayor isn't suffering from stage fright.

With the Mayor's permission, here are several gems from his Vancouver workshop:

I once met a man from Zeballos
Who caught fish in the deep and the shallows
He did have a flaw
With obeying the law
And ended his life on the gallows.

We came to Peninsula Brooks
To explore all the crannies and nooks
After some had set sail
The wind blew a gale
And caused us to shout out gadzooks!!

We landed at the beach of Kapouse
And decided to air our drysuits
Which when hung from a tree
For all travelers to see
Looked like pirates at the end of a noose.

I hear of a pirate called Schanck
Who's not yet robbed any bank
Those who know him agree
With some certainty
He's not likely to walk off the plank.

And so we were entertained through an eight-course meal of roast
chicken, sausages, corn on the cob, quesadillas, chicken potato
salad, fruit salad, lemon coffee cake, and berry pie.

All in all, fine dinner theatre on Armchair Beach.

Stats

Date: Thursday, 22 July 2010.
Distance: Seven point one nautical miles.
Speed: One point six knots.
Time: Cultured.
Spray factor: Significant.
Dessert: Lemon coffee cake and berry pie.

30. Canasta

Canasta. If you compared us riding windwaves in the bay to ocean kayakers riding coastal surf, that's what you'd say we were doing, playing a sedate game of Canasta to their wild Texas Hold 'em. But that's the way it is: you play the hand you're dealt from the deck of cards you have.

Launching out of Bruno's, Tug, Devil's Slide Doug, and I played back the same old options for the hand we'd been dealt: ride the ebb against a 10-mph Lewinsky to Red Rock or paddle abeam of the ebb and wind to Pt. San Pedro and then around The Sisters to Armchair. Same ol' same ol' are what those options were, like the deck was stacked against us.

Time for a new deck of cards.

Here's what we did: we paddled with the ebb against the Lewinsky across San Rafael Bay to the west end of the Richmond-San Rafael Bridge. Our reasoning for an hour-long struggle against wind-challenged water was a thing of beauty, as masterful as dealing from the bottom of the deck unseen.

At the end of the 2-mile crossing, we planned to do an about-face and ride the windwaves past Chard and Buckwheat islands to Dynamite Beach, 3 miles to the north. A 2-mile struggle in exchange for 3 miles of bliss.

San Quentin State Prison is the most notable landmark at the west end of the Richmond-San Rafael Bridge. But it isn't the only landmark. The second most notable landmark at the west end of the Richmond-San Rafael Bridge is the Marin Rod & Gun Club. Of the two named activities in the Club's title, only one remains: fishing, guns long since abandoned to the plow.

For those not drawn to fishing, the club offers a third alternative: a cozy bar. It was the bar, not the derelict fishing pier limping 700 yards into the bay, that snagged our fancy. Taking out at the Club's small concrete boat ramp, we elbowed up to the bar minutes before the barkeep called it an evening, ours the last drinks served.

The drinks we took outside to a green lawn, picnic table, and sweeping bay views. The only drawback was the Lewinsky. While we sipped our beverages, she switched from a fast jog to a steady walk, the windwaves we'd splashed over on our way to the Club now somewhat subdued.

Subdued, but not entirely gone. Jellyroll water with white frosting is what we had going to the club; glazed donuts with gently curved crowns is what we had going to Dynamite. A downgrade to be sure, but still quite pleasant, the rounded donuts and their shallow donut holes just deep enough for us to slide down, our boats moving forward with minimal effort.

Twelve years old, that's how old we felt cruising from the Rod & Gun Club across San Rafael Bay to Dynamite Beach. Not surprising, our fireside chatter on Dynamite segued to tales of our youth. Different tales for each of us, but all pretty much consistent with memories of our parents setting us loose summer mornings with the single admonition, "Get home before dark . . . but not too much before dark."

Those tales eventually wandered to today's equivalents of us then. Seems like the leash binding parents to their modern offspring is a lot longer, thicker, what with cell phones, Facebook, Twitter, and all the other fancy electronics.

One consequence of that electronic leash is modern kids seem overly protected, don't have as many opportunities to get down and dirty. We used to rip up our own Levi's playing, now kids have to buy them pre-ripped and torn because they can't play as rough and tumble (or so it seems).

If I don't come home from an evening paddle smelling of smoky campfire, Sandy inevitably asks if I really went paddling. That said, our campfire chatter inspired a new product as marketable as pre-worn blue jeans: off-the-rack clothes that smell like they've been played in all day. Sweat, smoke, grease, mud . . . lots of possibilities. Canned childhood smells don't have to be limited to clothes, either; they can be added to soaps, lotions, hair creams, topical medications, and what have you.

If you've got capital to invest in this lucrative and untapped market, don't hesitate to contact me. I'm the one who smells like a campfire.

Stats

Date: Wednesday, 28 July 2010.
Distance: Six point two five nautical miles.
Speed: One point two knots.
Time: Five point two five hours.
Spray factor: Decent.
Dessert: Chunky chocolate chip cookies.

31. Three Rum Beach

A big smile scampered across his face, the right corner of his mouth reaching up to his right ear, then the left corner of his mouth running the same race with his left ear. "I'd rather be where you are, not where I am," the smile said.

The smile sprinted across the face of a fellow in the passenger seat of a white pickup, gardening tools and Marin yard trimmings poking out of the truck's open bed. The pickup was on the west end of the Richmond-San Rafael Bridge, driving slowly, stuck in traffic. I was in my kayak, surfing a windwave toward the bridge, a smile to challenge the fellow's on my face.

That's all there was to our brief encounter, smiles all around, his truck trudging east on the low span, me gliding under and to the other side of the bridge on the last legs of that windwave.

Half an hour earlier, Marcus, Arch, Jay, the Czar, Sam, and I had put in at Danny's Secret Launch. A southerly wind imitating the high-pitched soprano of the Vienna Boys Choir in the harbor's rigging and a flood pushing north set our course for us, one we had no intention of reorchestrating.

Singing the same tune as the currents, the wind put more of a check on the waves than if the two had been going head to head. But at a constant 20 mph, the wind fetched up enough water to make the paddle to the bridge interesting. Leastways, the fellow in the white pickup seemed to think it was worthy of a smile.

As often happens, conditions on the north side of the bridge were in counterpoint to those on the south, the Choir quiet, the water flat. With no particular destination in mind, we sauntered

400 yards further north to the Marin Rod & Gun Club, hoping for happy hour cocktails, a repeat of last week's visit to the same club.

Instead of happy hour cocktails, we were served up disappointment. Not able to show proof of club membership, we were turned away, unlike last week. Even persuading a club member we met outside to accompany us back to the bar as guests failed to fill our glasses, the barkeep even less receptive to our pleas.

Disappointed but not discouraged (maybe just a little), we shoved off with dry whistles to see what we could find further north. As hungry as we were thirsty, the goal of our paddle now was to find a spot to take out, build a cook fire, and do dinner. We followed the riprapped shoreline 1.5 miles before we found a rock-free bight of sand large enough to handle our small fleet.

Our takeout was a secluded public beach. Small though it was, we shared the 35-yard-long by 15-yard-wide patch of sand with more than a handful of locals, our presence perhaps drawing a larger than usual crowd, their comings and goings not tapering off till nightfall, when we had the place to ourselves.

Our whistles in need of wetting, the Czar, immediately on landing, brandished three shot glasses and an equal number of masked rum bottles, our task to select the best of the lot. After several false starts and mandatory refills, we chose our winner. Of the three rums, now unmasked—Pyrat, Kraken, and Black Seal—Kraken took top honors with Pyrat a close second, Black Seal struggling to surface in third.

We eat well on our paddles, not a particularly well-kept secret. We've had salads and we've had salads, but never have we had a Caesar Salad garnished with chicken barbecued onsite over hot campfire coals. Thanks to Marcus for that one and everyone else for the sausages, soup, potato salad, and hors d'oeuvres.

On the water by deep dark, smooth paddling was ours to the Richmond-San Rafael Bridge, only minor splashing over our bows on the bridge's south side. I hear that Tomales Bay is bioluminescing, every nighttime paddle stroke and bow wake a light show. No such luck in San Rafael Bay Wednesday evening, though the red and green deck-light-lit spray over our bows had to be a close second, the spectacle as tasty as Pyrat Rum is to Kraken.

Stats

Date: Wednesday, 4 August 2010.
Distance: Six nautical miles.
Speed: One point three knots.
Time: Four point seven five hours.
Spray factor: On the south side of the Richmond-San Rafael Bridge.
Dessert: Snickers candy bars.

32. Pet Sematary

Ernie left Pet Sematary Beach on a tidal wave of sound, the muffler on his '84 Harley Davidson Electra Glide for show only. By deafening contrast, Billy Pilgrim slid through the water as quiet as a ninja, me not letting his black shadow out of sight from the Pet Sematary to Bruno's.

The reason I didn't let Billy Pilgrim out of sight the 4 miles from the Pet Sematary to Bruno's was because he and everyone else—Philippe, Phil, the Czar, Don't Follow Don, Sam, Jay, and Devil's Slide Doug—had left me behind on the earlier crossing. Left so far back I didn't make contact till I reached the Sematary long minutes after their takeout.

A forgotten spray skirt was the cause of my lonely paddle. The spray skirt was mine, and I forgot to tug it over my head at Bruno's. Fact is, I was in my boat, paddle in hand, ready to shove off the beach when I noticed my legs stretching into the Tern's forward recesses, the cockpit uncovered. Hiking back to the truck to retrieve the skirt left me 500 yards at the back of the pack.

That's 500 yards I never made up, not that I didn't try. The palms of my hands are still smarting from pushing hard against the Greenland paddle, trying to cut the distance between us. The harder I pushed, the further away everyone moved. Wasn't long before I couldn't see them at all. If I were Catholic, I'm sure I would've spent more time in the confessional explaining my abstract language to the padre than I did under the heat lamp warming my aching hands.

Despite the hurry, the day was perfect for paddling across San Pablo Bay: clear blue skies, warm without being too hot, just enough wind and current to give the water character. Perfect conditions, yet the only other traffic I encountered on the bay were a tug pushing a barge and two Vallejo ferries (Baskerville and Bruiser, thankfully no Cujo). For such a large body of water, the bay is a well-kept secret.

Leaving me behind on water but not on land, the lads waited on Pet Sematary Beach before they struck off on foot for Pt. San Pablo Yacht Harbor's Sportsmens Club. Q: Why did the kayakers cross the bay? A: To get to the Sportsmens Club. No joke. Fact is, anyone of us would've soloed across the bay to the Sportsmens Club, so I've no cause to complain.

One of two less-than-gentrified hangouts we frequent (Buck's the other), the Sportsmens Club and its harbor smack more of Jack London and Terry & the Pirates than it does of modern times and rotomolded plastic yacht clubs. So, imagine our shock and horror to find the door to the club locked, the interior dark through the front windows, empty as a zombii's tomb.

Disappointment, definitely disappointment. But short-lived disappointment. Working out front on the shock of his '84 Harley Davidson Electra Glide, barkeep and all-round good guy Ernie spots us fumbling at the door. Exchanging a key for the crescent wrench in his hand, Ernie walks past us to the door, which he opens with a welcome flourish.

Inside, Ernie flips lights, and we warm barstools. Two of the bar's spigots pouring Samuel Adams beer, light and dark, we fill our glasses, eat chips and fresh popcorn. Talk is about this and that, old and new, familiar and unfamiliar.

The launch from Bruno's at 5:30 PM and the crossing less than an hour, we're in the club by 6:45, give or take a few minutes because of my late start. We lollygag till 7:30 before traipsing back to the Pet Sematary, where we set up camp at the far end of the beach. We have permission from Eric, the harbormaster, to build a small fire. Using local tinder, our fire is cautiously small, Eric not a person to cross. Food cooking on the grill, Ernie joins us for dinner.

Here's what we have for dinner: vegetable soup, acorn squash cooked on the grill, barbecued chicken sandwiches, potato salad, and an array of hors d'eouvres. The main course is a more-than-large fire-roasted flank steak, courtesy of Phil. Dessert is French truffles and fire-warmed apple pie, whipped cream optional. The sun gone 2 hours, the moon moments ago, we break camp and leave, Ernie's big Harley growling inland, our boats sighting on distant shore lights to cross the dark bay. The sky is pincushioned with stars, the Milky Way erupting out of Sagittarius and arcing over our heads.

The stars I can see, but not the boats around me, Phil and Philippe in Phil's double, Jay and Don't Follow Don in Indiana's borrowed triple, Billy Pilgrim and Devil's Slide Doug in singles. Not of a mind to paddle alone across the bay in the dread of night, I latch onto and follow the nearest boat, Billy Pilgrim's, and that's where I stay till we reach Bruno's, tight as a bunion on a big toe.

Stats

Date: Thursday, 12 August 2010.
Distance: Seven point three nautical miles.
Time: Five hours.
Speed: One point five knots.
Spray factor: Some, not much.
Dessert: Apple pie and French truffles.

33. Gobsmacked

Gobsmacked. That's what we were—anyone who saw it had to be—gobsmacked.

Leaving Schoonmaker, the six of us—Billy Pilgrim, Billy's son Billy the Kid, Phil, Devil's Slide Doug, Marcus, and I—knew it was there 2 days past, but not if it lingered there this Thursday evening.

It was still lingering there, anchored ¼ mile offshore at the south end of Sausalito: a 390-foot-long super yacht owned by Russian billionaire, 38-year-old Andrey Melnichenko. The $300,000,000 source of worldwide boating (phallus?) envy appears at the top of everyone's alphabetized list of personal luxury yachts. The ship's name: A.

A bright lad, Melnichenko has degrees in physics and economics, his billions coming from more-than-wise investments in fertilizer, banking, and energy.

A successful businessman, Melnichenko. Problem is, I've been reading too many spy thrillers and can't help but question how a 38-year-old can become so rich without having founded a computer company or written the defining iPhone app. Call me old fashioned, but . . .

A doesn't temper my imaginings, the yacht cutting a hi-tech wake out of some futuristic James Bond flick. Pure white, the bay doppelgangering off its mirror smooth hull, the craft has a published top speed of 23 knots with a range of 6000 miles.

What the literature doesn't say is whether that top speed is above or below water, A designed with a suspiciously submarine look to its profile. The convex ax bow is most submarine-like, the clincher A's multi-storied superstructure mimicking the lines of a conning tower. Lots of glass in the conning tower look-alike, all said to be bulletproof.

The six of us paddled up to the ship's open tender bay, only one of two custom-built 30-foot-long boats still in the bay. Overseeing the remaining tender was a single crewmember, a young fellow who spoke English.

We chatted with the fellow about this and that, not getting too much info about this and that. Around 50 crew members and staff, ship registration was in Bermuda, itinerary included north along the coast, the helicopter that just landed on the bow didn't belong to the ship, it was just a convenience found at most ports, and so on.

Billy the Kid's 15th birthday, we asked if our crewmember friend could part with a glass or napkin with the ship's logo. "A birthday gift for the boy," but he said no, not that trinkets weren't to be had, but because he couldn't leave his post by the enormous open bay door (my speculation, not his admission).

I won't speculate how many hidden eyes and surveillance gadgets were trained on us, but if my readings of the spy genre are accurate, the six of us were well monitored. The kid we were talking to? Blackbelt in all the martial arts, fluent in a half dozen languages (inclusive of lip reading), a connoisseur of modern art and fine wine, a photographic memory, and no limits on his Diners Club card.

Leaving the tender bay and its multi-talented guard, we paddled around the ship, snapping Kodaks, no one stopping us, though we did spot a female looking down from the deck of the captain's bridge six stories up. "When's happy hour?" we shouted skyward, but her answer was a short Cyrillic laugh and she disappeared from the railing.

Our curiosity whetted, hardly sated, we paddled from A with a stiff wind at our backs over chunky water to Pallet Beach on Angel Island. We learned little of A on Pallet, mostly speculation and surmise, but we did sate our appetites with chili over cornbread, orange-flavored chicken strips, and the usual hors d'oeuvres.

Dessert was twofold: fancy peach halves warmed over hot coals and topped with whipped cream and cinnamon (Phil's creation) and a huge chocolate birthday cake for Billy the Kid, the cake not as immense as A, but so large we couldn't eat it all, the remains consumed by campfire.

Pallet thin when we landed half way through the flood, we left an hour before the beach did a James Bond, it thinning faster than the hair on the aging spy's pate. Only item of interest on the paddle back to Schoonmaker was a dull blue light (голубой, a color Russian scientists have given special attention to) glowing off A's hull. No doubt a secret low-frequency light-emitting tracking probe.

I love a good spy thriller.

Stats

Date: Thursday, 19 August 2010.
Distance: Seven point one nautical miles.
Speed: One point six knots.
Time: Four point five hours.
Spray factor: Da.
Dessert: Peach halves topped with whipped cream and cinnamon and a large chocolate birthday cake.

34. Time Travel

Billy!

No answer.

Hey Billy!

No answer.

HEY BILLY!

Still no answer.

Billy Pilgrim and I are paddling back to Jailhouse from Red Rock, leaving the Czar to overnight. We're about half way to Jailhouse, following the Richmond-San Rafael Bridge. It doesn't often happen, but it's happening tonight. The wind isn't settling down, the water isn't calming.

Nothing serious, not katywompus or breakneck. Nothing that my limited skill set can't cope with. Wind's a little less than quartering on us, waves and swells are well mannered, marching in straight rows, rarely capping white. Billy and I are sloughing in and out of the bay's shadows into light cast by the bridge's arc lamps, swells pushing us north, us ferrying south to keep a straight course.

We're paddling side by side, the smart thing to do at night in these conditions (smarter for me than Billy, his paddling skills way better than mine). Out of nowhere, a windwave running 90° to its mates snatches up Billy and shoots him ahead, parallel to the bridge, Billy stern-ruddering to keep straight. He gets a good, long ride. I paddle after him, closing only when his wave peters out.

Out of breath, I coast past Billy's boat, maybe half a boat length ahead, maybe a whole boat length before I ship my paddles, but not much further. I wait for Billy to pull alongside, thinking of something to say, something like, "Where'd that wave come from?" or "Nice ride." Small talk. But Billy doesn't pull alongside. I look back. I look left. I look right. No Billy Pilgrim. "Hey Billy" a half dozen times. No answer. I'm told the mind fills in missing gaps to complete pictures. My mind wastes no time filling the gap between Billy and no Billy.

Billy Pilgrim's namesake is the main character in his uncle Kurt Vonnegut's novel, "Slaughterhouse Five." That Billy Pilgrim time travels. That's the missing piece my mind fits in between Billy Pilgrim and no Billy Pilgrim: he's gone time traveling. A backup to that filler, I briefly entertain the possibility that Billy has been abducted by a UFO, that thought ignited by reruns of the "X-Files."

Despite his namesake's well-documented time traveling, Billy Pilgrim has not literally disappeared (nor has he been snatched up by a UFO). What has snatched him up is another wind-driven wave that carries him north under the bridge rather than parallel to it, Billy disappearing from sight in the bridge's thick shadow.

Not till he's milked the wave for all it's worth and come to a stop 45 yards to my right does Billy Pilgrim answer my shouts. We link up again, side by side, and paddle to Jailhouse without further incident, that despite nonstop wind and waves. The earlier going from Jailhouse to Red Rock encountered the same conditions, wind and waves the entire way, no dead zones.

From the evening's earlier paddle, two minor mention-worthy incidents. Rock gardening the west side of the island, Billy is beached by a surge on a partially submerged boulder and forced to walk his boat to the rock's edge. From there he seal launches successfully into the bay on a swell rebounding from the cliff behind.

Not much further along—between the large rock outcropping that hosts the abandoned Coast Guard fog bell and the island's south end—a surge sneaks up and scoots me sideways across the tops of three submerged rocks, a thunk on the bottom of my wood hull for each crossing. Not always my usual fate, I stay upright and paddle with Billy and the Czar to Toilet Bowl Beach.

(A brief aside on the superiority of wood vs. glass boats: After Thursday's paddle, Billy Pilgrim's glass boat is for sale. My wood boat is not.) Wind and waves, but you wouldn't know it sitting on the Toilet Bowl. On the island's north end, both beach and water are sheltered from southwesterly winds. The wind's only visible signature is campfire smoke swirling in lazy spirals over our makeshift camp. We hang around camp till our food and chatter run out. The Czar lays out a ground cloth for his sleeping bag, and Billy Pilgrim and I pack our boats for the paddle back to Jailhouse. Under an India-ink sky with a slightly nibbled-on full moon to light our way, we anticipate nothing but smooth paddling ahead.

Stats

Date: Thursday, 26 August 2010.
Distance: Five point five nautical miles.
Speed: One point four knots.
Time: Traveled four hours.
Spray factor: Plenty.
Dessert: Cream-cheese-filled coffee cake.

35. Irrefutable Logic

Billy Pilgrim and Bo spent the day paddling and kayak-surfing for 2 hours down the coast at Linda Mar before doing our evening paddle out of Schoonmaker to Angel Island.

I could be wrong about this, but I suspect the majority of the evening's 11 kayakers (except for Bo and Billy) would've liked to paddle up Raccoon Straits, around Pt. Blunt, and down to Pallet Beach. A pleasant evening with currents flooding up the Straits, that course (longer than the one proposed by Bo and Billy) made sense.

But sense doesn't always count, Bo and Billy both bellyaching about all the paddling they'd already done at Linda Mar, in between bellyaches extolling the virtues of a shorter paddle to Pallet around the southwest corner of Angel.

None of the rest of us—Zeerover, Jonathon, Don't Follow Don, Jay, VT Don, Indiana, StarMan, the Czar, and I—could argue their logic, their logic having nothing to do with distance paddled or sweat expended. Their logic was this: we've got the barbecued ribs and the chocolate fudge birthday cake (Billy and I sharing the honors but not the age, me with many more rings in my trunk); if you want to feast, follow us.

Truth out, I was coming around to their way of thinking. Not so much the food, but approaching Pallet from the southwest, that direction awash in well-formed and -behaved wind waves. The waves were fetched up by a blustery Lewinski steamrolling under the Golden Gate, the Lewinski herself not touching us, not messing with the waves under our boats.

The serious kayak-surfing Bo and Billy did at Linda Mar earlier in the day? I can't do that, I've tried. But the playful waves under us at the southwest corner of Angel, I could handle them.

Fact is, I was having such a good time letting one after the other of those well-mannered scooters carry me to Pallet, I forgot myself, got a little cocky, thinking, "Well heck, Linda Mar can't be any more challenging than this." And, "Bo and Billy, whata' they know?" Thoughts like that.

I said as much to Bo after we took out at Pallet, how Linda Mar couldn't be any tougher than what we'd just come through. Bo just arched his eyebrows, rolled his eyes back, and walked off.

Sharper than a chainsaw, that look of Bo's. Instantly cut my fragile ego down to size. I'm surprised no one shouted "Timber!" Fortunately, egos are easily inflated, mine with ribs and cake. Adding to the inflation were garden-fresh cucumber and tomato salads, roast chicken, macaroni and noodles, and watermelon.

The bay wasn't particularly warm, wasn't particularly cold, Jay, Indiana, and I each bodysurfing 5 minutes worth of the same waves we'd just kayak-surfed into Pallet. Only drawback was the Lewinski that fetched up those waves pushed a tube of fog across the city front, blocking what's usually an exceptional view from the beach.

The temperature nose-dived with the setting sun, long sleeves and pants replacing bathing suits as the preferred evening wear. Plans afoot among 5 of our 11 to overnight, those 5 (the Czar, VT Don, Bo, Jonathon, and Billy Pilgrim) jockeyed for the highest and driest spots on the beach as the evening darkened.

Billy Pilgrim got the coveted spot, between the upper end of the pallet and the bluff, all dry sand above the high tide line. A b'day cake diversion, that's how he finagled his spot. Billy made a show of the cake he brought, slicing it up, leaving the slices on the cardboard backing. While we busied ourselves fighting over those pieces, large and small, Billy quietly laid claim to that prized stretch of sand, no one the wiser.

Less paddling than I'd planned for with a few bruises to my ego, I can't complain about Thursday night. I even learned a thing or two: never compare surfing wind waves to surfing beach break and if you plan to overnight, bring a birthday cake.

Stats

Date: Thursday, 2 September 2010.
Distance: Six point four nautical miles.
Speed: One point three knots.
Time: Four point seven five hours.
Spray factor: Yes.
Dessert: Chocolate fudge b'day cake.

36. Campmor Catalog

Nothing beats a Campmor catalog for camping equipment: cookware, utensils, clothing, tents, backpacks, sleeping bags . . . But I don't want to talk gear, I want to talk paper, the paper the catalog's printed on.

Published on tissue-thin paper, two or more catalogs laid flat in a dry bag consume little space. That the catalog itself is sized smaller than the footprint of a dry bag makes it even more convenient, no folding or spindling necessary. If you're building a campfire and can't find natural kindling, you couldn't do better than lighting up a Campmor catalog.

Wednesday night—Wednesday night because Wild Bill's ceramic art show was Thursday and we couldn't miss that—found only two of us, the Mayor and me, on Armchair Beach. The Mayor the chef of choice in our two-man division of labor, the job of fire building was mine.

Dried twigs, the smallest thick as a kayaker's thumb, were plentiful. Smaller and more easily combusted tinder, however, wasn't. Dry leaves littered the ground, but no matter how many I stuffed under the pyramid of twigs I'd laid up, the pile didn't ignite.

At the bottom of my blue dry bag was the latest edition of the Campmor catalog, snailmailed to my home address. The complete unabridged edition, lots of paper. Crumpling pages, I started with shoe and boots, figuring leather and shoelaces would burn well. When they failed to ignite, I turned to tents, but the entire stock must have been coated in flame retardant.

A no-brainer, that's what finally lit my fire. Eight pages of propane and butane hardware worked like a torch: tanks, lanterns, stoves, conversion kits, hoses, grills, fuel adapters, and so on, the thumb-thick thicket of twigs ablaze in seconds.

Armchair Beach much visited, wrist-thick and larger longer-burning tinder have been used up. A downed eucalyptus on the beach's south end still has a few good-sized branches, but we lacked a saw to remove them. Scouting the beach's opposite end, I stumbled across a treasure trove of large kindling, nothing smaller than a pirate's wrist in diameter.

The find was propped upright and leaning against a small buckeye at the base of the bluff at the north end of the beach, just above the high tide line. Six 7-foot-long pieces, what looked to be a mix of scrub oak and eucalyptus. Each piece saw-cut on both ends. When the Mayor and I broke camp, we had kindling leftovers for another fire, maybe two.

Who cut the wood? We didn't do it. I suspected Tug; he often paddles alone out of Buck's, Armchair a frequent takeout. But it wasn't Tug, I called him and he said, "No," not him. With time and thought, I now suspect that stash of firewood has as much to with a stagnant economy as it does with campfires.

Paddling past McNears Beach on our way to Armchair we spotted three fisherfolk on the beach. When we left Armchair several hours after sunset, the same three were still in place, a small campfire burning. "You catch anything?" "Not yet," their shouted response.

Pastimes, McNears has been one of more than several public beaches we've been kicked off at sunset, sunset the outer limit for beach going. That these folks were fishing from the same spot well past sundown begs the question: Where were the rangers? Sacrificed to budget cuts?

Long story short, I figure the wood I found on Armchair was a byproduct of people fishing up and down the shore, time restrictions now unfettered by fully employed rangers.

Just as there are advantages to parks with underemployed rangers, so also are there advantages to small paddling turnouts. One is meal size. The Mayor and I alone by the Campmor fire, we two ate the six full servings of risotto with shiitake mushrooms and scallops the Mayor had prepared in advance for a larger group (the quantity no doubt influenced by last week's 11 paddlers).

One disadvantage of a small turnout is the potential absence of a favored food group. Neither of us brought dessert. No cookies. No chocolate. No cake or pie. We did have a bottle of wine, though not a dessert wine. But dessert as constant and necessary for us as green is next to blue in a rainbow, we'll call it a dessert wine.

A 2007 pinot noir, Miss Olivia Brion's label depicts a young lady riding a bicycle, yellow scarf flying from her neck, a French Poodle at her rear wheel, a large black locomotive spewing smoke and roaring close behind. The inscription on the back of the bottle:

"This wine is an homage to Olivia Brion, suffragette and descendent of a great French wine family. In 1905 Olivia, wearing long pants and short tresses, stunned the sporting world—and won a huge wager—by outrunning a locomotive from Canterbury to Maidstone. Later in life she ignited a furor by publishing passionate letters from her many paramours including; Jack London, Warren Harding, Paul Gauguin, Charles Chaplin and Isadora Duncan."

Our paddling time on the water was less dramatic than our time with Miss Olivia Brion. Going, the three of us (Sam paddling as far as the quarry) jounced lightly on cat's paws, The Sisters slightly more feisty, popping small champagne corks. Returning, it was the memory of Olivia—she sweeter than a cat's meow with a lingering aftertaste of barking poodle—that kept us awake on flat, mind-numbing water.

Stats

Date: Wednesday, 8 September 2010.
Distance: Less than Canterbury to Maidstone.
Speed: Slower than a speeding locomotive.
Time: Four hours.
Spray factor: Here and there, mostly there.
Dessert: Miss Olivia Brion.

37. Bioluminescence

India-ink black, a million flares of bright white tracing galaxies under my boat, explosions of concentrated light with long streaming tails intertwining.

What I saw in the water might've been the Milky Way reflected, the streamers of concentrated white remnants of the Perseid meteor shower. But Tomales Bay was smothered in a thick, dense federdecke of fog, stars and meteors memories from clearer nights. No starry reflections tonight. What I saw in the water was actually in the water.

Bioluminescence, that's what I saw, that's what was aglow in the water. A number of critters, marine and land, can luminesce—light up. The marine organisms responsible for the lightshow in Tomales Bay were single-celled dinoflagellates, a form of marine plankton. The critters are sensitive to pressure changes around them, a paddle stroke, a hand in the water, the bow wake of a kayak setting them off in paroxysms of delight.

Kayaks simply floating in the water Thursday night created enough pressure to ignite a Fourth of July. Sweep a paddle or hand through the bay and entire galaxies would supernova. Moving, the glow from individual paddle strokes luminesced for one or two seconds, leaving a trail of distinct footprints for each boat, small prints for narrow Greenland paddles, larger ones for bigger bladed whiteman paddles.

Each set of kayak prints followed an arrowhead of light, the boat's bow wake. The faster I paddled, the larger and brighter the wake. Year's past, we've kayak surfed the waves that stretch across the mouth of Tomales Bay. The faster we surfed, the brighter the light, waves breaking white spectacular.

Our takeout at Swing Beach 1.5 miles from the mouth, we could hear the waves breaking, calling out to us. But we didn't answer their call, not this time. Me? The earliest I'd respond would be January, the latest July. The rest of the year, the mouth of Tomales Bay belongs to Great Whites.

One corner of the infamous Red Triangle (the other two Año Nuevo and the Farallon Islands), the mouth of Tomales Bay is where Great Whites meet, greet, breed, and feed January to July. Not particularly interested in human tenderloin, the sharks fancy seal meat and the like. But they have been known to make mistakes.

Imagining the piercing spotlight a Great White ignites when he's heading my way is plenty for me, nothing up close and personal, please. Truth is, I'm completely satisfied with the shower of Perseids and their flaming tails much smaller fish painted under our boats at Swing Beach.

Exhilarating in Thursday's light fantastic were an odd baker's dozen: Dawn, VanMan, Gran'pa Pete, Danny, the Czar, Mary Ann, Jonathon, Sean, Dennis, the Mayor, Kane, Don't Follow Don, and I. The light drawing out a larger than normal crowd, we dined on a larger than normal meal. Two roast chickens, poached salmon (poached because we couldn't find a grill to barbecue on), lots of salads and appetizers, beer, chips, and dips. Desserts were chocolate fondue with figs and strawberries and apple pie with whipped cream.

Swing Beach, named for a swing that's appeared in many configurations over the years and hanging from a mammoth eucalyptus, has ample space for overnighting. Of our 13, 6 stayed the night, the Mayor, Jonathon, Sean, Dennis, Kane, Mary Ann, and Don't Follow Don navigating the heavy dark fog back to our launch site, Nick's Cove.

Swing Beach's eucalyptus is a monster tree. Biggest one I've ever seen. I slept well away from it, under a Bishop Pine. Danny slept under the monster's shadow. I woke the next morning dry and happy, the ground around me no wetter than morning dew. Danny came out of his tent haggard, big drops of water drumming his tent the night long, fog collecting in overhead branches to the tune of a waterfall, the ground around puddled.

Nearby San Andreas Fault excepted, Swing Beach, by my reckoning, has no faults. Thursday evening, the brightest concentration of bioluminescence I saw in the bay was in its cove. Friday morning, 7 river otters made an appearance there. Two years ago, a baby gray whale greeted us at sunrise in the cove.

The river otters well along on their journey to the bay's mouth (I suspect their lean body mass has little interest for Great Whites), the Czar and I packed up and headed back to Nick's Cove, the other five campers opting to spend the day on the bay.

Fog thicker than clam chowder, the Czar and I hugged the shoreline for 1.5 miles before crossing over to Nick's. A mile to go, we had few visual cues to guide us: no wind, no current, no sun (only a vague easterly glow), no visible land past Hog Island. Far as we knew, we were paddling in circles.

Pastimes, I've used a few iPhone apps kayaking: a ship finder, a tide tool, a wind forecaster. To this list I can now add the phone's built-in compass, using it the first time Friday morning to navigate our way through the gray to Nick's Cove, spot on.

That's it, there's no more to tell.

Stats

Date: Thursday-Friday, 16-17 September 2010.
Speed: Easy going.
Time: Enlightening.
Spray factor: None.
Dessert: Chocolate fondue and apple pie.

38. Four-Shoulder Paddle

Arch calls half an hour before I leave the house for Bruno's. "Bay's calmest I've seen in a while," he says. "Pretty nice day, too, real blue skies."

"You paddling with us?" I ask.

"Can't," he says. "Haven't got my gear," Arch on his way home in the south bay from a job site up north. "Wish I could, maybe I'll make the paddle next week."

"Hope so," I say, the call ending.

Not till I'm half way to Bruno's, my kayak taking up half the space on my truck's boat rack, does it occur to me I could've loaded my Mariner II for Arch and met him at the launch. Extra paddles, skirts, PFD, I had all those, too. I've got to get my gray matter's synapses realigned, tuned up, life going by at 90, them firing at 60.

Even if my mind had been running a click or two faster and Arch had made the paddle, I was doubtful we'd have as large a turnout as last week's 13 at Tomales Bay. "No way I'm gonna see that many," my real expectation running contrary to that thought.

September's nighttime ecliptic has been crowded with four big names: Venus, Mars, Saturn, and the longtime star of Virgo, Spica. As regular as your alimentary canal on Castor Oil, these four didn't miss a night, kiting across the sky as loose and limber as a laxative, all aglitter, seasoned performers to the end.

Only curtain calls now, the show pretty much over, the four moving on to new venues, the next big performer, Jupiter, the main headliner.

Rounding the last curve in Bruno's parking lot, even my low-octane mind grokked that last week's constellation of paddlers had moved on, too, a lone and solitary figure, paddle in hand, standing next to his van in the space closest to the put-in.

"Where is everyone?" asks Phil.

"Gone to Mendocino for BASK's big annual," I say.

"Ahhh," he says, "I forgot about that."

The evening's what Arch had phoned in: clear, calm, warm. Red Rock, to the south of us, is our destination. Reaching Buckwheat and Chard, Phil and I alter course, Phil on point with, "Let's ferry east across the current to Two Brothers and ride the ebb from there to Red Rock."

A gentle ferry angle, the bow's of our boats pointing just a few degrees north of the Brothers, we make good time, chatting the whole way about this, that, and related topics. The only shoulder ache of the evening—and a short, mild one at that—happened along the back side of West Brother, the ebb quite fast there, Phil and I paddling against it so we could round the island's north end and catch the main current accelerating through the channel between the Brothers.

The current between the islands moving at speeds I wish my mind was capable of flung us like pellets from a slingshot at Red Rock. We coasted in to Toilet Bowl Beach as the sun was setting behind the Richmond-San Rafael Bridge, two raptors hovering above the rock, waiting for their dinner to appear.

When all's said and done, the easiest course to Red Rock would've been the quickest, straight from Chard and Buckwheat. But, had we paddled that, our wait on the Toilet Bowl would've been 2 hours, the tide not flip-flopping until 8:30 from an ebb to a flood for an assisted return. Following the longer and more time-consuming course, our wait for the 8:30 departure was one hour, not two.

What the raptors dined on I don't know, but I imagine it was a meat dish, mostly protein. What we dined on was mostly carbs: papaya, vegan sushi (this is California, after all), chicken salad. If the raptors fed only on what we had for dessert, they went hungry. The evening's drink of choice was Arrogant Bastard Ale, three Bastards erasing any thoughts of the dessert we didn't have.

On the water past the Richmond-San Rafael Bridge by 8:30, we rode the flood, returning to Two Brothers en route to an updated course. Over dinner, we added the Sisters, 1.75 miles past the Brothers, to our must-visit list, seven islands more impressive a paddle than five.

September's original four headliners well belong the western horizon, Jupiter and a Full Moon took center stage. Two-thirds of a mile past Two Brothers, a blazing comet with a long tail cut for entertainment made a cameo appearance, entering stage right at Cassiopeia, exiting stage left at the tip of Draco's tail.

The Sisters were snoozing, no high leg kicking and flapping of white-laced skirts this evening. So calm were they, when threading Grindle's needle we were able to push our paddles straight down into the narrow passage without the current sweeping them away. For the curious, the passage was only three feet deep an hour into the flood, our paddles smacking solid rock.

More for the curious. This Wednesday was the autumnal equinox, the beginning of fall, roughly equal hours of light and dark, all following days till the winter solstice growing progressively darker. According to some sources, the full moon shone bright on the same evening as the equinox, those same sources claiming such an event—full moon on the fall equinox—wouldn't happen for another 20 years.

According to other sources, the full moon didn't shine till Thursday, one day after the equinox. Close, but . . .

In light of these discrepancies from varying sources, here're the evening's paddling stats. If you don't believe them, check their source.

Stats

Date: Thursday, 23 September 2010.
Distance: A marathon of paddling.
Speed: Impressive.

Time: Relative.

Spray factor: A blur at the speed traveled in the time given.

Dessert: Can't be described, has to be eaten.

39. The Log

"Burn it in half," this from Billy Pilgrim, a refrain normally voiced by the Czar. But the Czar's on a self-imposed month-long sabbatical, a month during which he cleanses his system by being respectful of authority, unopinionated, self-effacing, and careful to color within the lines. The Czar doesn't paddle with us during this time of cleansing, the prospect of contamination a strong deterrent.

"Burn it in half," Billy says, eyeing the telegraph-pole-sized log, the backdrop / windbreak for the evening's campfire. A foot in diameter and 7-feet long, the log is heavy, four of us barely able to drag it into place.

The Mayor spots the log anchored to the beach on the northeast side of Red Rock just before we take out on Toilet Bowl Beach. Not that the Toilet Bowl is shy of tinder and kindling—the beach is one of the north bay's major dumping grounds and has driftwood enough to feed the fires of Burning Man—but that log calls out to the Mayor, catches his fancy.

Towline in hand and Indiana to help, the Mayor hikes back to the log, secures it with the rope, and tows it into the bay. In ankle-deep water, he and Indiana walk the floating log to the Toilet Bowl, the scene reminiscent of photos I've seen of Russian dissidents in the Gulag dragging cut trees over snow-covered ground, ropes digging trenches into their shoulders.

No Gulag on Red Rock, the five of us—the Mayor, Indiana, Billy Pilgrim, Phil, and I—here quite willingly. No snow-covered ground either, the pebbly beach a bright red under Saran Wrap skies, an unblemished sun watercoloring long shadows. Ashore, the log is two or three hernias from its final resting place, those hernias avoided with four sets of shoulders and a towline stretched to its limit.

The campfire is a success, among the best we've had, the log a master windbreak and one evening's limitless fuel source. Burning hot, the fire needs minimal tending, minimal feeding. The campfire taking care of itself, we busy ourselves with dinner: ribs, fried shrimp, and a 4-tomato salad. Chicken salad and California rolls for hors d'oeuvres.

Midway through our meal, a lone kayaker paddles into view. We don't recognize the boat, we don't recognize the kayaker. He paddles onto the Toilet Bowl. I leave the campfire to meet him at the waterline.

"Do I know you?"

"I'm Mark," he says.

"Mark who?" I say.

"Mark from Tacoma," he says. "Jonathon emailed you about me, told you I wanted to paddle with you guys tonight."

"Oh yeah," I say, scratching my head, remembering. "How'd you find us?"

"A guy back at Jailhouse said he talked with you on the beach. You told him you were heading to Red Rock. He pointed the way, and here I am."

Introduced around, Mark from Tacoma blends in effortlessly, an easy fit to our fivesome, "Great fire you got going here" the clincher to our paddling bond.

Dinner shared, we turn our attention to dessert. Phil offers up chocolate-covered raisins, tasty placeholders while we wait for Billy Pilgrim's creation: marshmallow flambé. A simple enough sweet, ageless really, but taken to a new level of sophistication.

Using the campfire to its full potential, Billy pulls a bag of marshmallows from his drybag, we break arm-length twigs from tinder collected but not burned, spear the marshmallows, roast them over hot coals to a walnut brown, the sugary outer crust parchment-paper thin.

Traditionally eaten at this juncture, Billy Pilgrim introduces three new steps: 1) splash the roasted marshmallow with

Pyrat Rum, 2) ignite the rum over the fire, 3) top the flambé'd marshmallow with whipped cream. Exquisite.

Marshmallow flambé mellow, we pack to leave, the Mayor dousing the fire with two drybags of bay. The return to Jailhouse is much like the earlier outing to Red Rock, a quartering Lewinski confusing the water. Not Urban-Cowboy-mechanical-bull confused, more like the coin-fed quarter-scale bunking-bronco-in-front-of-the-local-grocery-store-when-I-was-a-kid confused.

For that level of confusion—and the marshmallow flambé—I'm grateful.

Stats

Date: Thursday, 30 September 2010.
Distance: Five point four nautical miles.
Speed: One point five knots.
Time: Three hours forty-five minutes.
Spray factor: Enough.
Dessert: Chocolate-covered raisins and marshmallow flambé.

40. Bojourn

Thursday morning, a message from Zeerover showed up in my inbox. Something to the effect of, "If the crew is so moved," sing happy birthday to the three names listed here when you buy your launch fees at Buck's. I can't remember Zeerover's exact words—they were in iambic pentameter—but that's the gist of it.

"Happy Birthday" was given voice, but the words didn't see the inside of Buck's, that fine institution locked up tighter than a diving bell when Phil, Don't Follow Don, and I showed up for the paddle.

Buck's locked door was our fault, the launch 2.5 hours earlier than normal and Buck's business hours waning as fast as daylight since the fall equinox. We launched early because of forecast wind and currents, our planned trip an 8-mile crossing of open water separating Buck's from Pt. Pinole. The earlier our put-in, the better the paddling conditions.

We did sing "Happy Birthday," even contacted several of the b'day celebrants via cell phone, but we did it at Pt. Pinole, a Sojourn of 8 paddlers adding their voices to our choir of three, a meetup with the Sojourn our motivation for crossing the bay.

The 8 Sojourners at Pt. Pinole were Bo, Laura, Andrea, Fran, KayakQueen, Herb, Paul, and the Czar, the Czar temporarily avoiding our Thursday night paddles while he cleanses his system of bad habits, fast-like.

The Sojourn's an annual week-long paddle lead by Bo to publicize Bay Access, "a 501©3 non-profit founded in 2001 by non-motorized boaters who wanted to ensure a future for the Bay that included adequate launching and landing facilities for human-

powered boats and beachable sail craft." More info at
http://www.bayaccess.org/ .

The East Bay Regional Park folks have laid out an open-air
campsite 100 yards from the takeout at Pt. Pinole. A grassy site able
to handle a good many tents, protection from the wind, picnic
tables, nearby restrooms, barbeque pits—a splendid place. Only
bellyache I have are park rules nixing beer and campfires. That said,
kudos to the East Bay Regional Parks for making the campsite
pleasantly available.

To overnight with the Sojourners or not to overnight with
the Sojourners, that was the question. "Yes" slowly morphed to
"No" as Thursday's initial count of 9 paddlers thinned in the days
before Thursday to 3. Following a Sojourner dinner of hors
d'oeuvres, hearty soup, and chocolate fudge cake, Phil, Don't
Follow Don, and I pushed our boats through ankle-deep boot-
sucking mud, first steps on our nighttime return to Buck's.

Low-tide mud behind us, the paddle to Buck's went
splendidly. The Lewinsky that soaked us earlier in the afternoon
with showers of spindrift and flying whitehorses had bedded down,
only an occasional nocturnal emission breaking over our bows. The
Vallejo ferries, Baskerville and Cujo, were absent, the water around
us no longer whipped into a frenzy by their too-close-for-comfort
passage.

We paddled under an evening sky that was bootjack-black
and crystal clear, sharp enough to whittle a Greenland paddle.
Rounding Pt. Pinole, an 8-mile crossing glowering at us, we could
see the lights at McNear's Quarry and Hamilton Field bookending
Buck's. Aiming for the spot bisecting the line connecting those
lights and just to the left of the last visible star in the handle of the
Big Dipper, we steered a true course.

We didn't meet up with Baskerville or Cujo, but we did
encounter a freighter-sized ship 3 miles from Buck's. We've had
close nighttime encounters with ships just as large, but this one was
going nowhere, it anchored in place by two large pilings driven deep
into the bay's bed and pumping slurry to Hamilton Field's wetlands
restoration project.

Several years back, we paddled out to a barge, several miles south of here, that feeds this ship the slurry it, in turn, pumps to Hamilton Field. The barge's crew weren't pleased to see us and sent us on our way with amplified squawks of disapproval.

No crewmembers on the large ship were up Thursday night to hurry us along, but there were plenty of squawks, a flight of seagulls that had settled on the water in the glow of the ship taking to the air in a flurry of displeasure at our passing.

The pumper and gulls 45 minutes gone, we took out at Buck's, the end to a most pleasant evening.

Stats

Date: Thursday, 7 October 2010.
Distance: Fourteen nautical miles.
Speed: Two knots.
Time: Seven Hours.
Spray factor: Quite a bit.
Dessert: Chocolate fudge cake.

41. Tupperware Photos

"Tupperware photos?" The question's mine and directed at a fellow on a 22-foot sailboat I'm drifting past on a slight flood.

"You know," he says, "all those photos you take year after year, and they start piling up? Well, my wife bought a big Tupperware container and stuffed all mine inside. I call 'em Tupperware photos, those old paper prints."

The sailboat's anchored 50 yards off Toilet Bowl Beach, the guy and a fellow sailor hard to see in the glare, the sun touching Mt. Tam's south flank behind their boat. A sunset photo op, I yank my digital camera from the pocket on my PFD and start snapping away, the current pushing me past the backlit sailboat.

"Whatcha' doin'?" he asks as I drift by. That question leads to our first exchange. My response is to soliloquize about all the digitals photos I shoot each Thursday evening (rarely less than 100) and how easy they are to store and sort through. That, in turn, segues into his Tupperware photo explanation.

My most recent sunset pics stored on a small plastic card inside my digital camera's metal housing (far more convenient than a Tupperware container), I bid the two sailors a pleasant evening and paddle ashore to the Toilet Bowl, the Czar, Jay, Don't Follow Don, and SF Dave in the midst of setting up camp.

The Toilet Bowl is never shy of wood, it a dumping ground for the north bay's hand-me-downs, driftwood prominent among the scattering. Adding to the mix of wood this evening, the Czar contributes a 2-foot-long, 1-foot-thick cut of bay tree plus several smaller cuts of redwood.

The combustibles are from the Czar's homestead, trimmed and downed to make way for sunlight to power solar panels Don't Follow Don's installing. To his credit, the Czar lugged all that firewood from Jailhouse to Red Rock by himself, in part because he's a nice guy, but also because none of us offered to share the load.

Large chunks of wood not guaranteeing a proper fire, a hatchet materializes in the Czar's hand as fast as you can say "Paul Bunyan," quartered kindling falling to the ground like pedals from a flower.

Our campfire is a fine affair, the quartered kindling burning bright and warm. The sailboat's still anchored off the beach, a small metal canister of charcoal briquettes glowing off the stern, just a glimmer of the gemutlichkeit at our camp. If I'd thought of it earlier—when I was snapping photos of the backlit boat—I would've invited the two aboard to join us for dinner. But I didn't, lack of foresight a poor excuse.

Dinner, by the way, is lots of sushi, a tossed green salad, a chicken salad-like dish with walnuts, pork loin, chicken nuggets. Dessert, courtesy of SF Dave's first mate, is a handful of homemade nano cupcakes and, courtesy of Don't Follow Don, an apple-berry pie, homemade from Trader Joe's.

During meal prep, a Coast Guard helicopter flies by, heading north. Before we quit the Czar to overnight on Red Rock, dinner plates packed away, a second Coast Guard helicopter skims over the top of Red Rock, also northbound. I don't know for sure, but I suspect the helicopters are participating in a Use-of-Force training exercise in San Pablo Bay, these events scheduled between 9 a.m. and 11:59 p.m. on random Tuesdays, Thursdays, and Fridays, every week of every month.

From the 6 November 2009 Federal Register: "The Coast Guard proposes to establish a permanent safety zone in San Pablo Bay for Coast Guard Use of Force Training exercises. This safety zone would be established to ensure the safety of the public and participating crews from potential hazards associated with fast-moving Coast Guard smallboats or helicopters taking part in the exercise."

The Register goes on to say, "exercises are designed to train and test Coast Guard personnel in the decision-making processes necessary to safely and effectively employ use of force from a smallboat or helicopter during Homeland Security incidents. The training will generally involve the use of several Coast Guard smallboats and/or a helicopter to intercept fast-moving, evasive target vessels on the water." The smallboats and helicopters fire ammunition, but they're blanks according to the Register.

Use of Force training exercises aren't scheduled for the stretch of water between Jailhouse and Red Rock (we crossed through Use of Force waters on last Thursday's paddle, between Buck's and Pt. Pinole). Returning to Jailhouse this evening, the only force on the water is academic, the surface as flat as a carnation folded in between the pages of a thick book.

Stats

Date: Thursday, 14 October 2010.
Distance: Five nautical miles.
Speed: One point four knots.
Time: Three point five hours.
Spray factor: None.
Dessert: Nano cupcakes and apple-berry pie.

42. Batman

Oow oow owooooooo!

Conventional Thursday night wisdom dictates that you howl at the full moon, on land and water. This Thursday's outing twists a wrinkle into that wisdom.

Bo, the Mayor, Jay, Devil's Slide Doug, Billy Pilgrim, and I launch from Danny's Secret Launch under a mottled gray sky threatening rain. An ebb flowing south to the Golden Gate, Angel Island calls out, a lonely wail at dusk, but not everyone hears.

Early morning Friday work calling out louder than Angel Island, a majority of our six opt for the closer and less-strenuous-to-reach Ferry Wake Beach, just north of Bluff Pt. on the Tiburon Peninsula.

Ferry Wake's naming is self-evident, more so when a high tide covers the beach and wakes are large. When we land on the sandy bight an hour after leaving the Secret Launch, the tide is out, a wake-dampening breadth of sand exposed between the water line and the backing bluff.

A night of celebration, we first toast Bo's birthday, he now eligible for Medicare. Next, plastic cups are raised to a first place win in Sunday's Sea Trek Regatta, Don't Follow Don, the Mayor, and I having navigated our triple around Angel Island before all other triples, our category win, "Oldest Combined Age in a Kayak." The Mayor garners additional kudos with his Bask Rodeo win. Emptying our bottle of Prosecco is Billy Pilgrim's certification as a Level III ACA Kayak Instructor.

Interspersed between toasts are fits of howling, the full moon painted in swirling grays and leering at us from behind scraggly branches. Even if you aren't inclined to howl, you can't help it. Not howling is not possible. Suffice it to say, riffs of primal yowling fill the night, outlasting even our campfire.

Before continuing this tale, a little background on Roman maritime law and property rights. Far as I can gather, current maritime law has evolved from ancient Roman law, which looked at rivers, bays, oceans, and such as avenues of commerce. To ensure that property owners bordering a body of water couldn't demand rights to or control commerce flowing by, Roman law set a specific boundary beyond which you couldn't claim ownership. That boundary was the annual average high tide line (average mean high tide line if you want to be nit-picky). Any beachfront below that line was legally in the public domain.

A handful of years ago we set up camp on a beach somewhat removed but still visible from a stately house. We were careful to keep ourselves below that line of lawful demarcation, the average mean high tide line. We explained all this to the deputy sheriff when he arrived, but he apparently was unfamiliar with ancient Roman maritime law and said in no uncertain terms that we were trespassing and had better leave. Pronto. We did.

This lack of scholarly understanding among beachfront homeowners and law enforcement has limited our nighttime activities to secluded and out-of-the way beaches. Ferry Wake is one of those beaches.

Or so we thought.

Standing around the last of our campfire Thursday night, the full moon having slid out of sight behind the bluff, we're wrapping up, kicking sand over the dying embers. From the south end of Ferry Wake, we see a small white light bobbing towards us. I do a quick nose count. We're all here, milling around the dying fire.

The light grows into a flashlight, a dark figure shining it on us. I count noses again, quickly. This fellow definitely isn't one of us.

"Where's your kayak?" I say, just to break the silence.

He doesn't answer, just shines his light onto what's left of our fire. Then the light's back on us. "This is private property," he says. "My private property."

Devil's Slide Doug starts to talk annual average high tide lines and maritime law, but he doesn't get far, me shaking my head "no," don't go there. I've got a bad feeling about this.

"How'd the fella get down here," I wonder. Not that I've done a thorough search, but I haven't seen any sort of trail down the bluff. The fellow's dressed like landed gentry, gray slacks, white dress shirt open at the collar, long-sleeved sweater draped over his shoulders, deck shoes. Clean as a raked lawn.

A fan, I've seen all the "Batman" movies, read the comic books. The fellow standing in front of us is a clone of Bruce Wayne, has that troubled superhero vibe, like he's looking right through you, sees everything, is ready for . . . whatever.

"The neighbors've been complaining about the howling," he says, his voice even, but marked with a not-so-hidden edge. "I don't mind the kayaks, but the howling . . . "

"We're done, sir," I interrupt, nervous, careful not to sound too bold. "We'll be gone in no time," all the while thinking about Bruce Wayne's martial arts training and his quick-to-flare temper. Yessir, we're outa here, discretion as honorable a capitulation as any swan song I could sing.

Bruce Wayne looks at me, looks at the ground, at his perfect deck shoes, hesitates, then mumbles "Okay," turns, and disappears into the gloom as quickly and quietly as he appeared. We're on the water a few minutes later, paddling back to the Secret Launch, the full moon at our backs.

It was involuntary, it really was, just like a sneeze, passing by the house we didn't see hidden in the trees on the bluff.

Oow oow owooooooo!

Stats

Date: Thursday, 21 October 2010.
Distance: Five point two nautical miles.
Speed: One point two knots.

Time: Four point two five hours.
Spray factor: None.
Dessert: Chocolate b'day cake.

43. Mudville

"Oh, somewhere in this favored land the sun is shining bright;
The band is playing somewhere, and somewhere hearts are light,
And somewhere men are laughing, and somewhere children shout;
But there is no joy in Mudville . . ."
    Casey at the Bat by Ernest Lawrence Thayer, 1888

      The Giants whipped the opposition in the second game of
the World Series. We watched the rout from our kayaks in
McCovey Cove, paddling from Ft. Mason's Gashouse Alley to the
ballpark. Truth be told, we couldn't see the game from the Cove,
but no difference, we were there for the party.
      That was Thursday, 24 October 2002. Today is
Wednesday, 26 October 2010. Besides the Angels being the Giant's
opposition in 2002 and the Rangers the Giants opposition in 2010,
there's one another major difference about this evening . . .
      Jay and I arrive at Bruno's within a few minutes of each
other. Two days before—Tuesday when I typically settle on a
launch site—I thought about putting in at Gashouse Alley and
paddling to McCovey Cove for Wednesday's ballgame. But a fierce
ebb would confuse the water on the return, and I wimped out,
fearful the water along the city front would be chaotic and a late
night pain in the paddle.
      Our regular launch at Bruno's rendered a Mudville after
harbor improvements, we set our boats down 20 yards further along
the water's edge and wait for our buddies to show. And wait. Only
one to show his face is Sam, but without his kayaking gear. "I'm

heading to a bar with a TV to watch the game," he says, and drives off.

Sam's departure leaves Jay and me the only two paddlers at Bruno's. The on-the-water launch time—5:30 PM—at hand, we shove off. Destinations more often than not last-minute decisions, we role-model Sam and set a course for the Sportsmens Club across the bay at the Pt. San Pablo Yacht Harbor.

Under #2 steel wool skies with a hint of orange peel at the horizon, we paddle the 4.5-mile crossing on water as tame as the Texas Rangers' bats. Not a hint of wind, our only challenge Cujo, and he steers a wide course around us. It's a good crossing, only to get better.

Far as we're concerned, the next best thing to being in McCovey Cove during a World Series game is to be in the Sportsmens Club during a World Series game. Heck, the Sportsmens Club might even be better, warm and dry, spigots flowing.

We talk it up on the crossing, what fun the Club'll be, the lights, the noise, the camaraderie, the hurrahs cheering the home team on. Not a night to be missed.

"Harbor's mighty quiet," Jay says, hauling his boat onto the Pt. San Pablo Yacht Harbor fuel dock. We're just a few berths down from the Club. "Dark, too."

"I think the blinds are pulled down at the Club," I say, squinting over my left shoulder. "Yeah, there's light poking out between the slats," not really believing it, my mind painting the last strokes on a picture I want to see.

We try the Club's front door. Locked. We walk around to the new deck in back, cup our hands against the sliding glass door. Look in. Dark. Where the glow from the TV should be, nothing. The long bar we figured we'd have to fight our way up to, empty. The rousing hurrahs, silent.

"But it's a sports bar," says Jay, like his saying it will make things right.

"Yeah," I say, my mind out of paint and brushes. "Wanna paddle back to Bruno's, see what we can find?"

We do, but the only thing we find is Mudville—landing at the old takeout, forgetting about harbor improvements, the suck on our shoes. We talk about watching the last of the game at San Rafael Joes, but that thought's stomped out by spotlights from the distant ballpark, just then celebrating the Giants' victory.

The Giants have won, but there is no joy in Mudville—Jay and I have struck out.

Stats

Date: Wednesday, 26 October 2010.
Distance: Seven point eight nautical miles.
Speed: Three point one knots.
Time: Two point five hours.
Spray factor: Just the tears in our eyes.
Dessert: Mud.

44. Tactile Delight

Two things. First a correction to last week's report, John G. pointing out that the Giants faced the Angels in the 2002 World Series, not the Dodgers as I mistakenly wrote. Second's not a correction but an addition, Chuck G. (not related to John G.) noting that Ernest Thayer, San Francisco Bay area local and author of "Casey at the Bat," fancied his Mudville after Emeryville, a small town bordering the bay across from San Francisco.

Speaking of San Francisco and baseball, the Giant's recent World Series win was heralded Thursday night with a lightshow. As we paddled across the east end of Raccoon Straits at sunset, the western sky exploded orange, the color mirrored iridescent along the entire breadth and length of the straits. The surrounding landmass black in the glare, the combination matched the Giant's team colors: orange and black.

The sky was spectacular, too, leading up to that sunset. An unseasonably warm evening, the sky defied the weather, looking like an ice hockey rink, thin, wispy white clouds radiating out haphazardly from the center, scratches from ice skate blades scoring the surface, cracks and deeper furrows criss-crossing here and there. Smooth swaths of ice populated the perimeter, the work of a Zamboni.

If sunset hadn't been imminent, I think that ice-resurfacing Zamboni would've machined those clouds into a non-tribute, washed the color out of the sky. But it didn't, the sun exploding gold from the sinking center of the rink, glowing deep orange upward and outward.

The water was in stark contrast to the sky. Smooth and blemish free as the dark lenses in Lady Gaga's designer sunglasses, it mirrored the balmy, warm temperature as truthfully as the colors. Mirror smooth, but soft like the proverbial baby's butt (I'd say Lady Gaga's, but I have no personal experience for that comparison), the synthesis of baby soft and mirror hard resolved into a delightful medium for paddling.

The colorful sky lasted only a few minutes, but the weather and water were constant the entire evening, the six of us—Don't Follow Don, Billy Pilgrim, Jay, Sam, Phil, and I—in shorts and t-shirts from start to finish. Only one bordering on complaint was Don't Follow Don, he having just that afternoon purchased a brand new dry suit. But he didn't complain, knowing that if he'd imprisoned himself in the watertight outfit, he'd have baked his apples by paddle's end.

We met Phil at Pallet Beach, he having paddled straight away from his boat in Sausalito. The campfire was laid up when we arrived, but not lit, a situation Billy Pilgrim quickly resolved. Low tide, Pallet was wide and inviting, the only drawback the smell of decay, the source a mystery. A gray whale beached itself several coves west of us 4 or 5 months ago, but we figured that wasn't the tangy odor's source, the beast's bones bleached clean white (one large rib having migrated to Pallet).

Over a meal of fish in the style of fish 'n chips without the chips, mixed veggies and shrimp, sausages, the regular hors d' oeuvres, berry pie, and almond thins, Phil regaled us of his just-returned-from Baja kayaking expedition. Turns out the focus of the trip wasn't kayaking, but his 1991 Suburban.

Kayaks, gear, and girlfriend loaded in the Suburban, Phil set off to join up with friends in the Baja. Before he could cross the border, the Suburban's rear end died. Equipped with 4-wheel drive, the van limped into a nearby repair shop on its front wheels, was put back together, emptying Phil's wallet in the process.

Skip ahead several days, Phil, the Suburban, the girlfriend, and his buddies on the roughest of Baja's backwater roads. The rear end dies again, only a banana stuffed into a transmission fluid outlet keeping the van alive. Inching onward, the group finds a repair shop, the owner a former licensed Ford mechanic. "Those mechanics in the states," he says, "they did the rear end all wrong," and does it correctly, the final bill less than a fifth of the first.

Phil, the girlfriend, and his buddies did get in some kayaking, but 4 days less than they had planned. The moral of this story? Phil no longer has a use for the Suburban, but he figures you might. If you could use a 1991 Suburban 1500 with 4-wheel drive, a new rear end, and less than 400,000 miles, give Phil a call. He might even throw in a bridge.

That said, we paddled back to our respective destinations, Phil to Sausalito, we to Danny's Secret Launch, the water brilliantly bioluminescent the entire stretch around Angel Island, the bursts of light fading to nothing the closer we got to the takeout.

An exceptional evening.

Stats

Date: Thursday, 4 November 2010.
Distance: Eleven point four nautical miles.
Speed: Two point three knots.
Time: Five hours.
Spray factor: Nothing.
Dessert: Berry pie and almond thins.

45. A Slight Push

Riding a rollercoaster over long slow loop de loops, that's how it's been the last month. I'm not talking about paddling conditions, though that's certainly part of the mix. It's the weather that's been up and around and down and about.

Thursday's paddles have been at the top of the coaster's track, long stretches of flat rail, our last few outings on flat water under warm skies, the skies clear to middling. Days in between paddling, however, have swung low into deep troughs of cold and wet.

Bookending paddles, two of our regular Sunday mt. biking pedals have been in downpours, the last downpour a week ago. This Sunday we rode to the coast in mid-80 temps. Dropping a relatively new singletrack in the headlands (Dias Ridge), we had spectacular views of the Pacific. The coastal water was as flat and calm as a pre-pubescent Lewinski, a small-for-this-time-of-year surge sprinkling the coast's rock gardens.

Thursday's paddle was in conditions similar to Sunday's pedal, only difference was temps in the low 70s rather than mid 80s. Nine paddlers showed up at Bruno's, six taking to the water, three remaining shoreboubd, their mt. bikes in the bed of Indiana's truck. Seeing us off with Indiana were Baja Rob, up for a short visit from Costa Rica, and Wild Bill.

The six putting paddles to water were the Czar, Jay, Zeerover, Billy Pilgrim, first-time Thursday nighter Liz, and me. Thinking maybe we'd navigate our way to Armchair Beach, Billy Pilgrim changed those plans with, "Let's see what the new gal can do. How about crossing over the shipping channels to the Sportsmens Club, see how she handles the dark and the ebb."

Liz handled conditions well, though the ebb wasn't as swift as we thought it'd be. The only boat to come near was Cujo, his junkyard-dog behavior at bay, leaving plenty of room between us and him when passing. If winter weather ever descends on a Thursday night outing, Liz can show her stuff then.

The Darkening upon us—Standard Time displacing Daylight Saving Time last Sunday—we launched from Bruno's at 4:30. Despite that early put-in and a less-than-strenuous 4-mile crossing to the Sportsmens Club, we reached Pt. San Pablo Harbor knee deep in dusk, the sun long since down at 5 PM.

Wasn't just our takeout, Pet Sematary Beach, that was muddled in dark, the Sportsmens Club was dark, too, darker than a WWII London blackout. To quote Yogi Berra, "Déjà vu all over again," the club locked up just as tight 2 weeks ago when Jay and I paddled over to watch the World Series.

Dejected but not without hope, we meandered along the rusty railroad tracks that lead past the club, walked down the three wood steps to the front door, and tried the doorknob. The knob didn't turn, but a slight push on the hand-worn ball swung the door back on its hinges. We stepped in, turned on the lights, the switch by the door. All was as it should be, minus local patrons.

Billy Pilgrim took command of the bar, three of four taps on the fritz, but one working all we needed. Wasn't until beers were poured that the evening's local barkeep arrived, not surprised to see us, our presence filtered to him through the harbor grapevine. We stayed long enough for refills, harbor updates, and the newbie to pay for our indulgences before heading back to Semetary Beach and dinner.

Semetary so named for a small flowered-and-stuffed-animal rock memorial to a departed pet on the beach's west end, we set up camp immediately opposite. An excess of sushi was complemented by salads (green and potato) and a skillet of fried potatoes, beans, and mushrooms. Dessert was chocolate-covered Bing cherries and – molded seashells. Pre- and post-dinner aperitifs were served up by Zeerover, potent double shots of sangrita and tequila.

Strong as the aperitifs were, they didn't take the edge off our launch from Sematary, that through a 25-yard stretch of mud we can only guess how deep. Billy Pilgrim gondoliered his way through using his break-apart spare paddle, walking the blades through the mud on either side of his boat. I skateboarded out, one knee in the boat, the opposite foot sluicing through bay gunk. The other four shouldered their boats to the harbor proper and launched from a mud-free dock.

The return to Bruno's equaled the going to the Sportsmens Club, unseasonably fine.

Stats

Date: Thursday, 11 November 2010.
Distance: Seven nautical miles.
Speed: One point three knots.
Time: Five point two five miles.
Spray factor: Zip.
Dessert: Chocolate-covered Bing cherries and chocolate-molded seashells.

46. Special Delivery

"Like a red morn that ever yet betokened, Wreck to the seaman, tempest to the field, Sorrow to the shepherds, woe unto the birds, Gusts and foul flaws to herdmen and to herds." –*Venus and Adonis*, Shakespeare

Shakespeare ever so thickly literate, the layman's common translation reads, "Red sky in the morning, sailor's take warning." The backside of that addage forecasts "Red sky at night, sailor's delight."

It's the backside that affects most Thursday night paddles. Till recently, sunsets over the bay have been humble, lackluster. Nothing to write home about. That's changing, two of our last three sunsets worthy of Priority Mail, this last Thursday's verging on Special Delivery.

Thursday the sun winked out just to the south of Mt. Tam, leaving Marin's highest landmark cast in dark shadow. Radiating out from the silhouetted mountain, a stage show of parallel bands of bright yellow to rich orange to dark purple tightly packed cotton balls filled the sky. Words don't do the event justice; you had to be there.

Only three of us—Don't Follow Don, the Czar, and I— bore witness. The rest of the regulars were honing their skills in Pt. Richmond's indoor saltwater natatorium. Why you'd launch your boat indoors rather out's a total mystery to me.

No, not a total mystery. I can think of at least one explanation: cold. Those same clouds (altocumulus) that lit up the sunset also sucked in a cold front, last week's nighttime temperatures in the low 60s plummeting into the 40s Thursday eve, the enclosed natatorium a warm exception.

Forecast literate, we three were prepared for the cold. Rather than the t-shirts and shorts of the last several weeks, the Czar and I wore wetsuits with spray jackets. Don't Follow Don wedged himself into a new drysuit, tight as a ship in a bottle. The Czar and I were comfortable enough paddling not to complain, Don't Follow Don too hot in his sealed terrarium not to.

With barely a breeze to ruffle the water, the 3-mile crossing from Jailhouse to Red Rock went without a hitch, the water at its worse a surface mimic of the cotton ball sky. We took out on Toilet Bowl Beach an hour past sunset, our headlamps lit well before the campfire.

Dinner was an herbivore's delight: steamed broccoli, vegetarian sushi, potato salad, pumpkin pie with optional whipped cream. Three our number, fireside chatter was monolithic, too few of us to split off into smaller conclaves. Don't Follow Don full of a recent tome on the Roman Empire (I forget the title), his book report dominated our discussion.

Much ado's been made about the country's parallel to Rome, the good and the bad, the ups and the downs. We got into that, talking military misadventures, political intrigue, public spectacles, popular dissent, and so on. Sensitive to class divides, we devoted a more than modest amount of time discussing the relationship of Rome's well-to-do to the not-so-well-to-do (with a special focus on slave girls).

In a high wind, you could spit from Toilet Bowl Beach to a place where that relationship might someday sink new roots. The Guidville Band of Pomo Indians some years back proposed a $1 billion Las Vegas-style casino with an 1100-room hotel, nightclubs, restaurants, and so on at Pt. Molate, a small abandoned harbor and mud flat just north of the Richmond-San Rafael Bridge on the Richmond side.

The local government was keen on the proposal, the revenue generated through taxes a potential gold mine. The locals, however, were less than enthusiastic, wary of the baggage—both well-to-do and not-so-well-to-do—that gets carried onto these flights of fancy. "Not in my backyard" their lament.

This last election, Measure U asked voters if they approved or disapproved of the proposal. More disapproved than approved. Nonbinding, the Measure doesn't nix the proposal, just gives voice to the body politic. Whether the well-to-do powers that be listen is anyone's guess, the rest of us slaves to their decision.

Stats

Date: Thursday, 18 November 2010.
Distance: Out and back.
Speed: Better than average.
Time: A fair amount.
Spray factor: Minimal.
Dessert: Pumpkin pie.

47. Alone

"You think I'm full of myself, in-your-face pushy, don't you?" says he.

"I never said that," say I.

"You don't have to," says he, "I can see it in your face. Just cause I'm short, you equate me with that weird TV fellow you find so amusing."

"You mean Cal Lightman? The lead character on "Lie to Me?""

"Yeah, exactly, that's what I mean."

"That is so wrong, I've never likened you to Cal Lightman."

"Give it up. You treat me like I'm here only to amuse you. Truth is, it's all a cover to hide the shame you feel for your inadequacies."

"What're you talking about," I say, averting his gaze to stare at my feet.

"What am I talking about? Did you paddle out to The Sisters tonight? Tell me that."

"I tried, but the ebb was too strong. I couldn't make headway, so I went back in to shore where the going was easier."

"'Where the going was easier'! That's so typical of you. I bet you didn't spend more than 5 minutes trying to reach the Sisters."

"That's all the time it took to realize I wasn't getting anywhere."

"What was it, 20 minutes later when you were heading back in their direction, the ebb going your way? Did you visit them then?"

"You know I didn't, you were there. You heard the waves breaking, you knew how dark it was. It would've been irresponsible to paddle into that."

"'Irresponsible' is what I hear, but shame is what I see smudged on your face. You know you don't have the skills to handle water like that, and you don't do anything about it. That's what's irresponsible."

I have nothing to say to that.

"And that dumb move you made at McNears," he says without missing a beat. "How stupid was that?"

"What're you talking about?"

"You trying to sneak onto the far end of the beach after sunset but paddling past the ranger's house with your deck lights blazing, that's what I'm talking about. And you acting surprised when that ATV came roaring down the beach with it's spotlight on you, and you not even outa your boat, yet. Jeez."

"Those deck lights aren't that bright, the ranger couldn't've seen 'em. Something else gave me away. Had to have been."

"Right. Sure. You're not thinking that maybe that Coast Guard helicopter circling all night had anything to do with it, are you?"

"Well, it fits. That helicopter also explains how the rangers at China Camp knew I was heading their way after McNears, why they were waiting with their truck headlights pointing out to where I was in the water."

"You're not only missing a string of lights on your tree, you're arrogant as well. A Coast Guard helicopter interested in you, following you all night, alerting local authorities to your presence? My oh my, aren't you the important kayaker."

"I never said I was important."

"Not in so many words you didn't. But what were you trying to do, huh? Poach a public beach closed for the night? Break the law, that's what you were trying to do. You're so important, you're above the law? Is that it?"

"Well, I didn't break the law, I never went ashore on those beaches. You've got that all wrong."

"Do I, now? What about Chard? The entire island's off limits day and night. Tell me about that."

"Hey, I had to do a T & P, my bladder was bursting, I was thirsty and hungry. I was only there 10 minutes, tops 15."

"You keep making excuses, but you're only fooling yourself. You keep it up, this won't be the last evening you paddle alone. I'm not the only one who sees through you, you know. You're as transparent as a broken beer bottle."

Paddling alone in the dark has certain meditative aspects, but listening to the rants of the stubby storm paddle lashed to my deck isn't one of them.

Stats

Date: Tuesday, 23 November 2010.
Distance: Eight nautical miles.
Speed: Two point three knots.
Time: Irritating.
Spray factor: Didn't get anywhere near it.
Dessert: None.

48. Tragedy on the Bay

Liz, Phil, and I were Thursday's paddlers. Launching from Jailhouse under gray skies and an ever-so-slight misty drizzle, we paddled out a few strokes from the beach before deciding on our destination.

I'd earlier toyed with the idea of paddling against the ebb across San Rafael Bay to Dynamite Beach at the quarry. The return to Jailhouse at evening's end against a flood, the consensus that never was shifted from struggling with currents in favor of an easier ferry across currents to and from Red Rock.

The bay was a gray plain, its horizon lost to an equally gray sky, the water flat, without texture. The storm that was forecast didn't happen, just intermittent drizzles. Red Rock's appeal for me were the manganese mineshafts; had the rain come, we could've sheltered inside one, laid a fire, cooked dinner in calm. I'd done it before, years ago with Devil's Slide Doug. It was cool. I'm sorry it didn't rain Thursday night.

Liz borrowed my Mariner II for the paddle. She's testing boats, looking to upgrade her fleet. The Mariner's a good-sized boat, nearly 18-feet long, lots of storage in the bow and stern. Among the gear Liz stowed in the Mariner was a big bag of kindling, all but a small campfire's worth burned on Toilet Bowl Beach. The leftovers we stashed in the poison oak behind the beach for a future fire.

Despite the Mariner's vast storage, Liz told me it wasn't enough. "Totally inadequate for women with baggage," she said. Note: It was into this same model of kayak that Jay stuffed a week's worth of food and gear for trip in the San Juans several years back, a folding full-length lounge chair he'd pushed into the bow forgotten until he unpacked at trip's end.

With wood aplenty, we lingered on Toilet Bowl over a slow meal of roast fowl, steamed broccoli, and a potpourri of hors d'oeuvres (California rolls, salad, cheese and crackers). Trader Joe's Dark Chocolate Sea Salt Caramels topped off the meal.

The last-standing privately owned island in San Francisco Bay, Red Rock, wild and untamed, was, at one time, ground zero for a major development. In the 1980s, a developer set out to tame it, proposed a top-tier 10-story hotel with casino and yacht harbor.

San Francisco, Marin, and Contra Costa counties, each laying claim to the 6-acre rock, were unable to agree on who would get what percent of the take. That disagreement plus sticky state and environmental red tape undid the developer's fantasies. The island's owner, now in his 80s, has since disappeared into Southeast Asia, taken a young Asian bride, and turned his other fantasies into the buying and selling of diamonds. Put on the market in 2006 for $6.5 million, Red Rock today lists for $22 million.

Aside from a decommissioned Coast Guard fog horn on the rock's south end, the only remnant of civilization on Red Rock is buried in the crushed red chert not far from our campfire: a white porcelain toilet, à la Franc. The toilet 2 feet under, Phil dragged his boat directly over the grave when we launched from Toilet Bowl Beach for the return paddle to Jailhouse.

End of summer there was a light bloom of bioluminescence in the water around Red Rock. No such phenomenon this Thursday night, though we did have a short-lived light show of a different variety.

The water—as flat and featureless as when we'd earlier put in at Jailhouse—mirrored the Richmond-San Rafael Bridge lights in long, straight, lifeless rows. The wake from a passing Vallejo ferry stirred the reflections to life, glowing snakes slithering in unison toward the bridge under our boats. You had to be there.

Ferries, wakes, and snakes . . . that pretty much wraps up Thursday's paddle. But not quite. Thursday's paddle didn't really wrap up until Saturday

Years past, we've twice quite by accident paddled into the quarry's holiday party. A large white tent pitched just around the point from Dynamite Beach, the festivities are hard to miss from the water. Uninvited, we've been welcomed both times, salt water dripping from our wetsuits and neoprene skirts not an issue.

Friday after Thursday's paddle, I contacted a source who knows a source who knows when this year's holiday party will be held. On Saturday, I received an email with the details.

While Liz, Phil, and I were eating streamed broccoli on Toilet Bowl Beach, the quarry was serving up champagne, beer, wine, and silver platters of fancy finger food and more in a big white tent just around the point from Dynamite Beach.

Stats

Date: Thursday, 2 December 2010.
Distance: The wrong way.
Speed: What's it matter?
Time: Misplaced.
Spray factor: Hardly.
Dessert: Dark Chocolate Sea Salt Caramels.

49. Two Boats

A warmish late fall day—the high 62° an hour before our launch, 60° when we put in at 4:30—Schoonmaker was all ours, no one else there to share it with. Nine boats on the empty beach, one a piece belonging to Billy Pilgrim, the Czar, Indiana, Jay, the Mayor, Phil, Sam, Liz, and me.

Of the nine boats, two were new to their paddlers: Liz and Billy Pilgrim. Liz, in the throws of purchasing her first real kayak, showed up with a Pygmy Tern, same vintage as mine, wood, 14' long, 23" beam.

Fact is, I knew that boat intimately, Gristle and I having built our Terns side-by-side on my patio in 2003. Gristle, graduating to longer skin-on-frames, sold his Tern a couple years later. Now, here it was again, back on the market and a Thursday night paddle. Imagine that.

Billy Pilgrim's already got more boats than he knows what to do with. A master-level paddler, he cartopped a borrowed sports car of a boat, a 15' 5"-long 22.5"-wide plastic Delphin, to Schoonmaker. Designed for maneuverability and playfulness, the vessel's ideal for rock gardening and surfing in conditions most of us work hard to avoid.

From Schoonmaker, we planned to head straight for Pt. Stuart, the Point on the southwest end of Raccoon Strait. An ebb forecast at 3 knots promised 30 minutes or so of easy surfing along that stretch of strait. Our intent was to paddle to Pt. Stuart without diversion, and we managed to do just that. For 100 yards.

In a bay of calm, the little harbor just south of Schoonmaker was whitewater, Class III or IV. Wind (there was none) and current had nothing to do with the foaming turmoil. A rampage of diving pelicans was the cause. Despite a number of us lacking skills for Class III or IV whitewater, we ventured into the fray.

The pelicans paid us no heed, cannon-balling within feet of our boats, the spray coming off the water as thick as you'll find with gale-force winds. Herring I believe were the cause of their crazed behavior, mid December right for the start of the Bay's herring run. Commercial herring fishing not slated to commence till 2 January 2011, the pelicans were taking advantage of that late start to catch their quota without commercial competition.

We braved the pelicans till the sky turned a pallet of gauzy pastels—sunset yellow, rose pink, burnt amber, magenta, purple—then broke free and resumed our trek to Pt. Stuart. The delay with the pelicans may have been the reason, but there was no surf to ride when we reached the Point.

I'm guessing Billy Pilgrim may have been more disappointed than any of us at the calm. Master and commander of many boats, the Delphin was new to Billy and, having already run it through its paces in rough water the day before, I think he wanted to see if it added any excitement to tamer conditions, though not as tame as what we found ourselves in.

Billy ordered his new Delphin a week or so ago, but it hadn't yet arrived for Thursday's outing. How he found himself in the Delphin he was paddling's an interesting story. The Clif Notes version would read something like this:

Four extremely competent paddlers go out the Gate. They trade boats to see which they like best. Billy trades his Sportee for a Delphin. A humongous sleeper wave smashes into the paddlers. The kayaker in the Sportee is sucked out of his boat, the Sportee disappears, the kayker swims ashore, walks the 3 miles back to the launch. The three remaining paddlers search for Billy's Sportee, but it's gone. No pieces, no nothing. Somewhere, Davey Jones Locker is having a sale on used Sportees.

That's the Clif Notes version. Here's the movie (titled 101208 Golden Gate Rock Gardening, tucked away at the end of the first write-up): http://paddlecalifornia.blogspot.com/.

In case my wife is reading this, I do not kayak in conditions like that. Trust me. I am a reasonable person. No, strike that last statement. But do trust me.

No rides at Pt. Stuart, we R&R'ed at nearby Kayak Kamp, feasted heartily (cauliflower curried in coconut cream, stir-fried rice, lintel soup, pork loins, tri-tips, a slew of hors d'oeuvres, chocolate cake), commented on life, and paddled back to Schoonmaker.

Stats

Date: Thursday, 9 December 2010.
Distance: Out and back.
Speed: Lackluster.
Time: Excellent if you were a pelican.
Spray factor: See above.
Dessert: Chocolate cake.

50. Relations

"Don't you know a storm's coming?" this from a dog walker on the breakwater at Bruno's. "Yeah," we say, but don't think it'll arrive till well after paddle's end, which is what happens. No storm, no rain on our outing. No warm temps, either: 46°F on the way to the Sportsmens Club, 44°F on the return to Bruno's.

With winds averaging less than 7 mph (in our face going, at our backs returning), maybe an occasional 10-mph gust, the water's placid, but you can feel the tension building just below the surface. The bay's waiting to do a Raging Bull, but that doesn't happen till early the next morning, the Bull goaded on by a Lewinski riding in on a fast Pineapple Express.

Truthout, the only blemish on an unremarkable crossing to Pt. San Pablo is the ship traffic. Besides the regular comings and goings of Cujo and his brethren, a traffic jam of tugs, barges, and tankers clogs the bay. Never a real threat, most spot us before upsetting our comfort zone, the faster boats changing course, the more massive putting spotlights on us so we change course. All told, our crossing takes 20 minutes longer than usual, stopping and waiting demanding a toll.

Liz, Billy Pilgrim, the Czar, and I take out at Pet Sematary Beach. One hundred eighty yards from the Sportsmens Club as the seagull flies, we're encouraged. Last two trips to the Club, we've been welcomed by dark windows, locked doors, and an absent barkeep. Tonight, from where we've beached our boats, we can see a yellow glow warming the Club's windows.

Better than the warm glow, the Club's front door is unlocked, and Jedd, the interim barkeep, welcomes us. Asked if the tap is pouring Sam Adams, Jedd answers with a tall glass of foam, an inch of amber liquid hiding below. We drink our beer from bottles,

Jedd at a loss for the empty kegs, filled only last week and "not that many showing up at the club since then to drink."

Warmer than outside, the building's interior is still on the cool side. The Czar offers to fire up the wood stove, and he and I lug in two armfuls of firewood from outback. The wood catches quickly, and, not long after, the metal stove's glowing rose. The Club, a large open hall, takes a while to heat.

Before the interior is completely warmed, the Club's de facto barkeep, Ernie, arrives, Jedd his stand-in. A cold 40-minute motorcycle ride from Santa Rosa painted red on his face, Ernie keeps his big black leather jacket on. In the short time it takes us to lament the absence of tap beer and Ernie to say it's the CO_2 cartridges that dispense the beer and not the kegs that are empty—the remedy a hand pump—the club's warm enough to dispel the red from Ernie's face and the thick jacket from his body.

"It's a small world" is a worn cliché. I'll say it anyway: it's a small world. The Czar and Ernie are related. This they discovered only recently. Not twins separated at birth and lost to each other, but in large extended families lost to each other, Ernie is the brother of the mate to one of the Czar's younger brothers. To each other, Ernie and the Czar are relations (relatives-in-law?) for want of a better term.

The Sportsmens Club now in the family, we dine inside, out of the cold, heating the evening's meal on a commercial-grade stovetop in our kitchen. The food we share with Ernie and Jedd, Jedd a close friend of Ernie and, therefore, family (a friend-in-law). Over sweet potato fries, soup, chicken salad, chips, and cookies with whipped cream, we talk extended families and share off-color Irish golf jokes.

The fire in the wood stove outlasts our stay. Goodbyes all around, we leave the warmth of family for the cold of Pet Sematary Beach and our boats. Despite the temperature, we're comfortable in our close-decked boats, few passing ships to slow a paddle to Bruno's just fast enough to keep our blood flowing and our noses and fingers warm.

Stats

Date: Thursday, 16 December 2010.
Distance: Seven point two nautical miles.
Speed: One point one knots.
Time: Four point seven five hours.
Spray factor: None.
Dessert: Cookies and whipped cream.

51. Unusual Behavior

Unusual behavior for us, knocking on the door of a beachfront McMansion to alert the homeowner we'll be settling in for several hours on the sand adjacent to his. Liz, the one knocking, not in synch with our m.o., not that familiar with our interpretation of California maritime laws and property rights (you can't restrict access to property below the average mean high tide line).

Lawful, that's what we'd be camping below the average mean high tide line, no neighborhood alerts necessary. Of course, pastimes we've been there, done that, ended up talking to police and beachfront property owners, both groups interpreting California maritime laws differently than us.

Even though the McMansion homeowner on Ark Beach tells Liz he has no problem with us stirring up his neighbor's sand (Liz had earlier in the week garnered access permission from that neighbor) and offers his grill for food prep . . . I just don't know. Being so responsible even though our interpretation of the law is so strongly on our side just seems irresponsible. But who am I to say?

Despite my misgivings on our excessive civility, the outing is quite pleasant. Wedged between two rainstorms, Thursday is on the cool dry side of the barometer, wind absent, water a polished lens. Fact is, in the short 2-mile paddle between Danny's Secret Launch and Ark Beach, the only wobble in the water we five—Liz, Eric, the Czar, Sam, and I—face is at Pt. Chauncey, that the consequence of a passing passenger ferry.

The ferry passes 150 yards out, none of us paying much attention. What does catch our attention several minutes later are slow-moving waves breaking our way, 50 yards distant. We paddle out to greet them, their friendly response long rides toward shore. Hoping for more, we 180 and paddle back out.

The wakes from the ferry peter out when we get into position, the water again flat as a slate pool table. Before we turn back to shore, two ferries, each going opposite directions, cross paths 100 yards farther out. We wait for the wakes and surf them to shore, but they aren't nearly as large and well formed as the first set, not quite as fun to ride.

I would've expected the combined wakes of two ferries to out-wake a single ferry, but that didn't happen. No nautical engineer, but I'm guessing a boat's propulsion system, hull design, cruising speed, and so on account for the difference in wake configuration. Next time passenger ferries pass, I'll pay more attention to the boats and the wakes they churn up.

Ark Beach, the end of our surfing session, used to harbor a large barge, positioned pretty much in the same location as the current home on whose door Liz knocked. The barge, home to a family of ceramic tile makers, was on the beach when I first paddled by in 1998. Six years later, in early 2004, the barge was gone, up and vanished.

Actually, the fellow who answered the door Liz knocked on had it removed so he could build his home. The old and showing-signs-of-dry-rot barge house was large, maybe 5000 square feet. Its replacement, a two-story Mediterranean-style villa, out-does the barge in both looks and living space, the villa tipping in at 6500 square feet.

Used to be, we'd stop at Ark Beach and speculate on when the bay would slosh over the barge's ground floor sliding glass doors. The villa's architects claim that'll never happen with the new building, watertight it is and will remain. But we're still speculating, figure rising sea levels plus the perfect storm will one day see us surfing ferry wakes into the villa's living room.

Excepting ferry wakes, this paddle is Liz's design. Besides garnering permission to hang out on Ark Beach and pre-empting the neighbor's fears of a ragamuffin beach invasion, the dry kindling that started the campfire was hers, a lug from the Secret Launch. The folding chairs that circled the campfire? Yeah, that, too, but not a lug, a nearby find.

Thursday the night before the night before, we wish you all happy holidays. May your ferry wake landings be safe and your below average mean high tide beach outings carefree and happy.

Stats

Date: Thursday, 23 December 2010.
Distance: Three point five nautical miles
Speed: Zero point nine knots.
Time: From a barge to a Mediterranean villa.
Spray factor: Wakeful.
Dessert: Mochi, raspberry-pomegranate ice cream, Christmas cookies.

52. End of Year

His landing looked like a sure thing, but it was a "Dewey Defeats Truman" misdirect. Ten yards from Pallet, a sneaker wave caught Zeerover from behind and rolled him over faster than Truman's surprise dumping of Dewey in the 1948 presidential election.

Unlike Dewey, Zeerover didn't concede upset, instead righting himself with a dignified handroll off the submerged sand and continuing the last 10 feet to shore under his own power. Though his recovery was more dignified than the pouting history records for Dewey, Zeerover did suffer material loss, his hat and prescription glasses casualties of the dunking.

That little wave was a surprise, the 3.5-mile paddle from Schoonmaker to Pallet Beach in benign conditions. Flat water, no wind. Only counter to that a shadowy silhouette of a gray whale nosing out of the water midway to Raccoon Strait. The gray broke the semblance of calm because it wasn't, the nose the bow of an upended skiff sunk by an out-of-control Lewinski less than 24 hours earlier.

The big Lewinski and the little sneaker wave, "big" and "little" both highlighting the bay's unpredictable nature. Might've been a third highlight Thursday, long slow swells as tall as a sunken skiff rolling into Raccoon Strait from the Golden Gate. "Might've been" because nothing came of them, the water laser-level flat when we reached the south side of the strait 1 mile later.

An aside on Raccoon Strait and an apology. I've always referred to the body of water that separates Tiburon and Angel Island as Raccoon Straits. It's only one strait, not two straits. I apologize for 10-years of misinformation. Though I've never given voice to it in these reports, I've always assumed the strait was named after the raccoons that terrorize picnickers and campers on

Angel Island. That was a false assumption. From the almost reliable Wikipedia:

"In 1814, the British, 26-gun, sloop of war, the H.M.S. Raccoon [ed. note: more often than not spelled Racoon], was damaged off the coast of Oregon, but managed to stay afloat long enough to reach San Francisco Bay. From March 13 to 19th of that year, the ship was repaired on the beach at Ayala Cove on the Northern portion of Angel Island; the present day ferry boat dock. This event is commemorated by the name given to the deep-water channel between Tiburon and Angel Island, now spelled Racoon Strait."

Wikipedia, almost reliable except for the spelling referenced in the last sentence. Given that, I don't feel so bad about my own misinformed spelling. Strange how that works.

Paddlers enough to field an off-season baseball team, Sam, Billy Pilgrim, Bo, Jay, Phil, Tug, Zeerover, Liz, and I crossed Raccoon Strait on our way to Pallet Beach. A large contingent generally equates to food aplenty. Spread across the large wood pallet at the east end of the beach this Thursday were barbecued ribs, pot roast, mushroom fettuccini, chicken salad, roasted red pepper and crab bisque, roast chicken, lintel soup, California rolls, and a well-appointed salad. A large sampling of chocolates and cookies claimed dessert.

The night crystal clear, San Francisco's tourist attractions—the waterfront, business district, Alcatraz, Golden Gate and Bay Bridges—filled the horizons to the south and east. Overhead were winter's constellations: Taurus, Aries, Pisces, and Aquarius along the ecliptic. Counting backwards around the North Star were Perseus, Cassiopeia, Andromeda, Pegasus, Cepheus, Cygnus, and Draco.

A cold evening, we clustered around the campfire from landing to launch. Kindling burned were milled wood scraps courtesy Liz and downfall courtesy the previous evening's storm. Past paddles, we've stashed unburned wood on various beaches for future outings.

We considered the same for Pallet, stashing a cache. But stepping away from the fire to prep our boats was a chilly effort, and our departure was delayed by the time it took to combust the remaining scraps. Wood consumed, the next warmest place was sprayskirted into our boats and underway, more than enough body heat generated by moving boats through water, which we did to Schoonmaker.

That's it, the last Thursday paddle for 2010. Here's to a happy new year and more paddles in 2011.

Stats

Date: Thursday, 30 December 2010.
Distance: Six point three nautical miles.
Speed: One point four knots.
Time: Four point five hours.
Spray factor: Only Zeerover knows.
Dessert: Chocolates and cookies.

ComiX

Giving a different spin to the Thursday night paddle reports are a series of comics that accompany each tale. What follows is from the 4 November 2010 outing.

JAY, SAM, BILLY PILGRIM, PHIL, DON'T FOLLOW DON, & I HAVE A COLORFUL TIME ON THE WATER. -- 11.4.10

BILLY PILGRIM CHECKING THE TIDES ON HIS IPHONE.

DESPITE ALL THE MUD, THE EBBING CURRENT DOESN'T GO SLACK FOR ANOTHER 3 HRS.

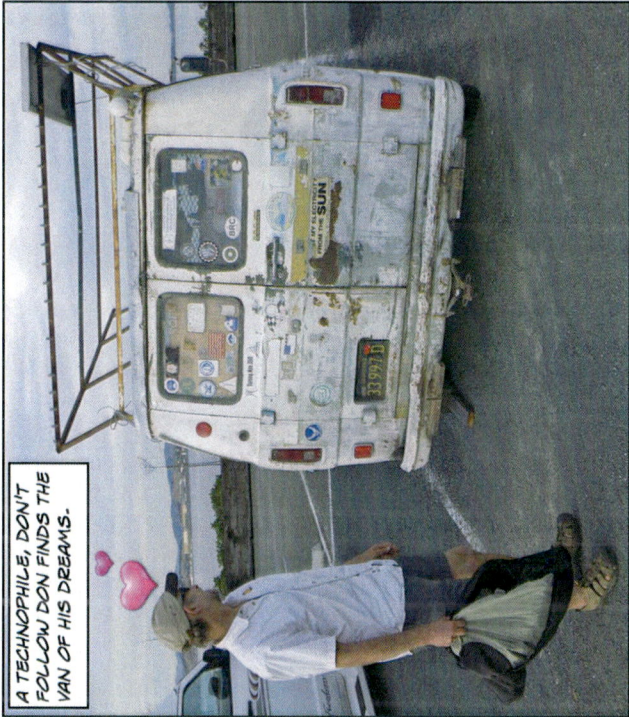

A TECHNOPHILE, DON'T FOLLOW DON FINDS THE VAN OF HIS DREAMS.

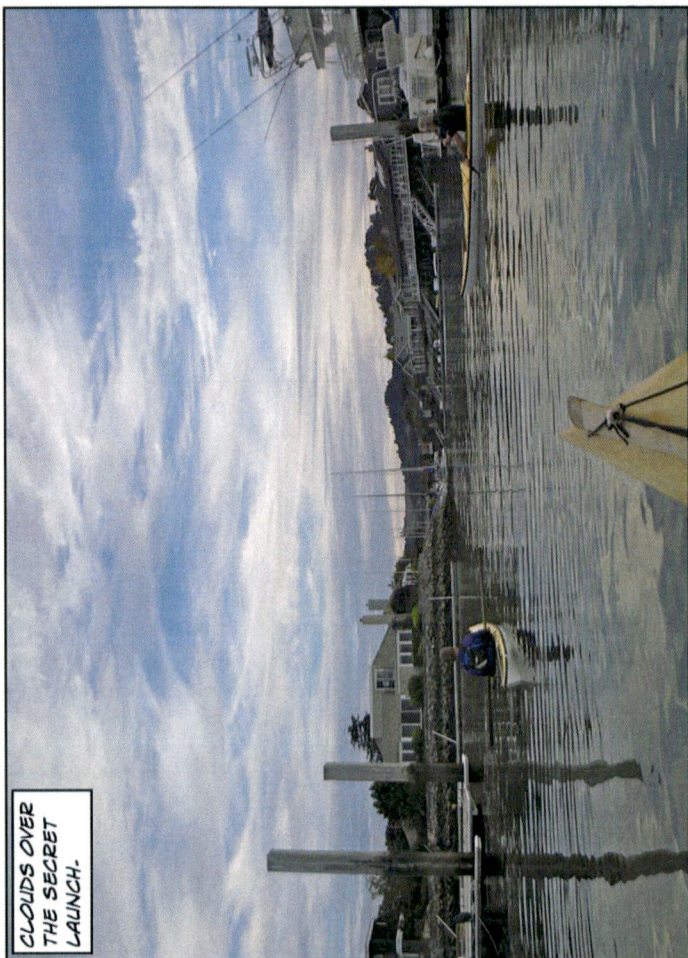

CLOUDS OVER THE SECRET LAUNCH.

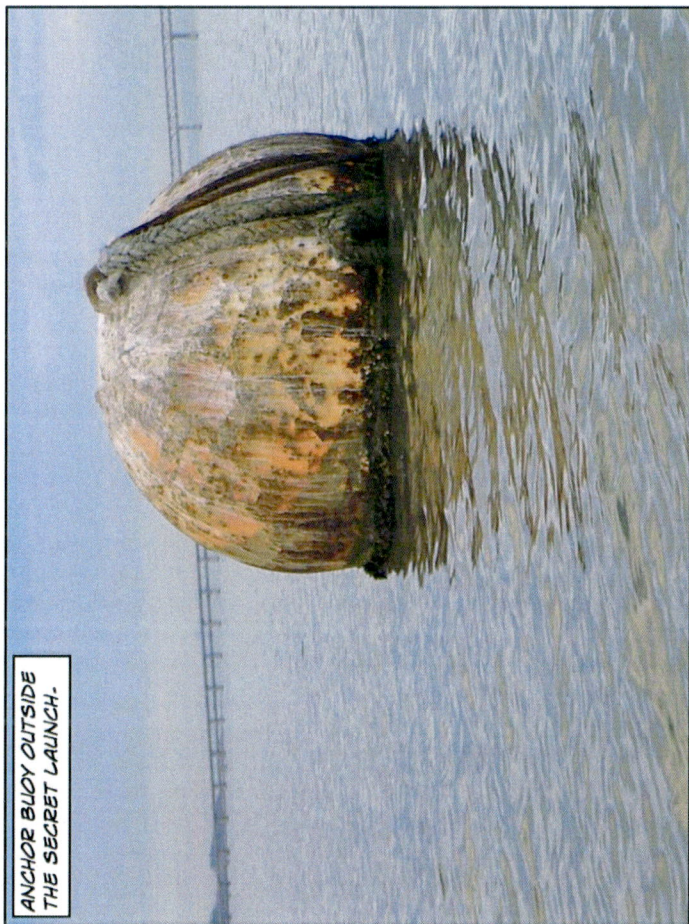

ANCHOR BUOY OUTSIDE THE SECRET LAUNCH.

A CAMPFIRE TO MATCH THE SUNSET.

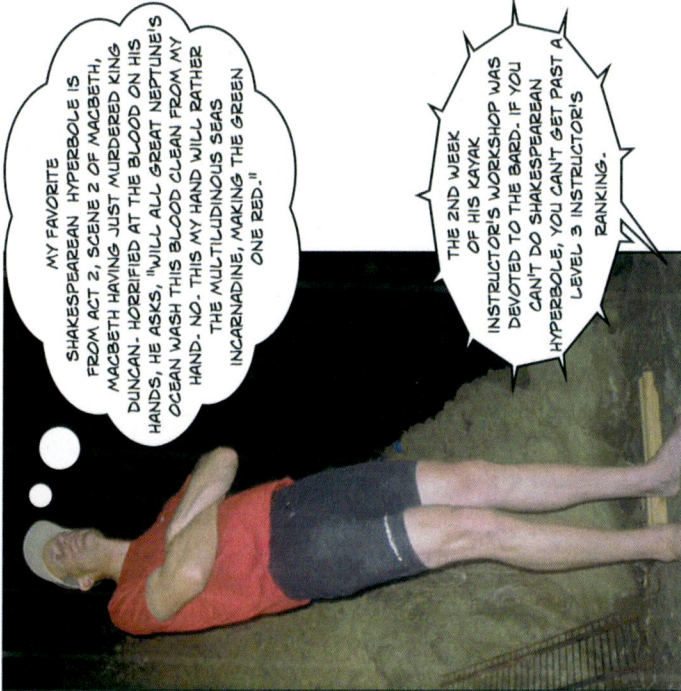

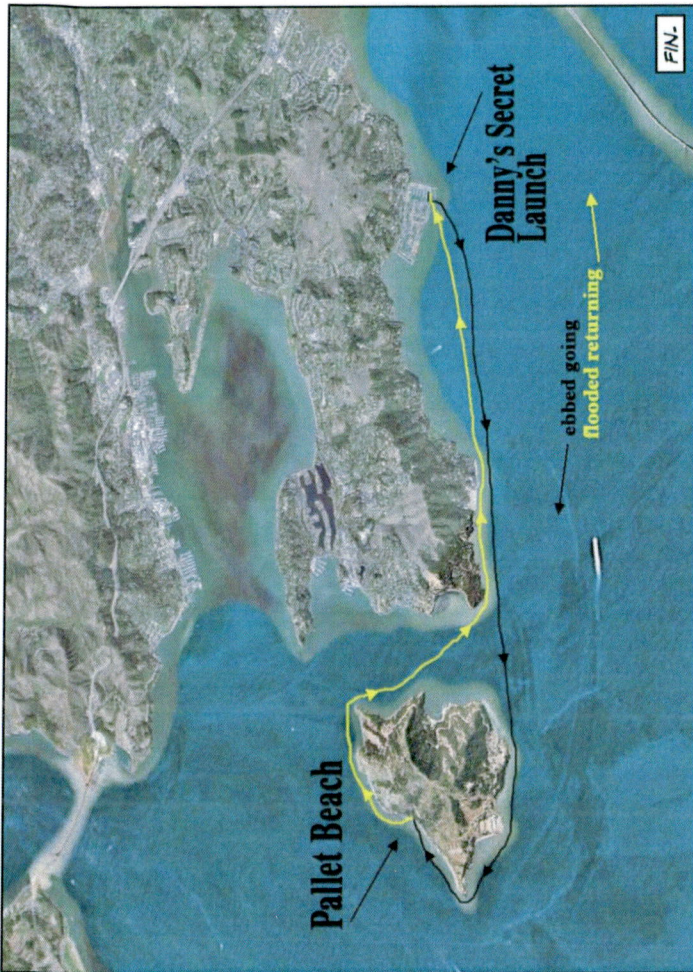

The author and his boat.